GUIDES

COOKING WITH HERBS

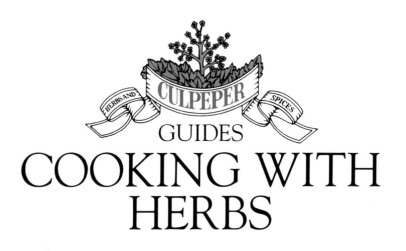

GUIDES
COOKING WITH HERBS

PATRICIA LOUSADA

General Editor
IAN THOMAS

Webb & Bower
MICHAEL JOSEPH

First published in Great Britain 1988 by
Webb & Bower (Publishers) Limited
9 Colleton Crescent, Exeter, Devon EX2 4BY
in association with Michael Joseph Limited
27 Wright's Lane, London W8 5TZ and Culpeper Limited
21 Bruton Street, Berkeley Square, London W1X 7DA

Designed by Ron Pickless

Production by Nick Facer/Rob Kendrew

Illustrations by Rosamund Gendle

General Editor Ian Thomas

Text Copyright © 1988 Patricia Lousada
Culpeper Trade Mark Copyright © 1988 Culpeper Limited
Design and layout Copyright © 1988 Webb & Bower (Publishers) Limited

British Library Cataloguing in Publication Data
Lousada, Patricia
  The Culpeper guides cooking with herbs.
  1. Food : Dishes using herbs. Recipes
  I. Title
  641.6'57

  ISBN 0–86350–211–3

Typeset in Great Britain by P&M Typesetting, Exeter, Devon

Colour reproduction by Peninsular Repro Service Limited, Exeter,
Devon

Printed and bound in Italy by Amilcare Pizzi SpA

CONTENTS

INTRODUCTION

It is hard to imagine what cooking would be like without the unique flavours provided by herbs. For centuries they have played an integral part in many of the world's great cuisines and today with the explosive interest in food from all corners of the world the range and importance of herbs is widely realised. In early civilisations herbs were also extensively used for medicinal purposes and this also is happening increasingly today.

Until recently cooks have had to make do with very few fresh herbs, such as sage, parsley and thyme. But the herbs available for the cook now include basil, coriander, chervil, tarragon, rosemary and dill. These and other fresh herbs are available throughout the year since they are imported from warmer climates. Methods of drying herbs have improved, and freeze-drying yields the best results. Thyme, marjoram and bay dry very successfully but most of the others will lose some of their character and fragrance, and are vastly superior when fresh.

Herbs are at their best when they are young and freshly picked, so it is well worth growing your own. They are charming plants, attractive to bees and butterflies. Most are easy to grow and will flourish if a little care is taken to find the right spot for them, often in the sun. They will also thrive in window boxes and indoors, but will need good light. The selection of herb seeds is exciting and increasing steadily. Herb mixtures or individual herbs can be chopped, packed in small yoghurt pots or foil packets and frozen. Sprigs of herbs can also be frozen loose, then stored. These will make a useful standby.

Herbs have an added attraction for the health-conscious cook. They are a wonderful boost to low-salt diets and possess intrinsic healthful properties. Most are packed with minerals and vitamins, some aid digestion and many stimulate the appetite.

Although there is a lot of scope for the creative cook to experiment, certain herbs are known to enhance certain foods. Basil and tomato, rosemary with lamb and fennel with fish are perfect examples. Other delicious combinations are roast chicken stuffed with fresh tarragon, and dill sprinkled over steaming new potatoes.

Classic dishes from France and Italy, where the culinary value of herbs has always been appreciated, can now be tackled with confidence thanks to the current choice of fresh herbs. There is no need to be slavish to the quantities recommended in any recipe. Herbs vary in strength of flavour and should be adjusted accordingly. You may also want to experiment with blanching herbs before using them. This will not only soften the leaves but will also mellow the flavour.

The versatile herb can impart its flavour to vinegars and oils, breads and soups, stuffings and sauces, salads and sorbets and subtly awaken our sense of taste.

NB *Quantities*
Ingredients in the recipes are given in metric and imperial measurements and the American cup system. The metric is given first followed by the imperial and American cup measurements in brackets. When measuring ingredients follow one set of quantities but not a mixture.

The cup is 8 oz, half the American pint of 16 oz. One tablespoon is 15ml; one teaspoon is 5 ml. Spoon measurements are level.

GLOSSARY OF HERBS

ANGELICA

Botanical name: *Angelica archangelica*
Family: Apiaceae (Umbelliferae)

This giant perennial looks very like a large cow parsley and can grow to a height of eight feet. It is best known today by its bright green candied stalks, but the entire plant, including the roots, is used medicinally as an aid for digestion. Perhaps that is why the stalks find their way to the top of cakes and puddings! It is also worth knowing that if you add some young angelica stalks to rhubarb or gooseberries they will counteract the acidity and less sugar will be needed. (About 25g (1oz) angelica leaf stalks to 450g (1lb) of fruit.) It is used in the making of liqueurs or aperitifs such as Chartreuse and Vermouth, and in combination with juniper berries by gin distillers. In Finland the stems are eaten after being baked in hot ashes and the Norwegians use the root for bread.

Angelica possibly got its name from its supposed celestial powers; many believe that an angel identified it as a cure for the plague and its name could bear witness to its strength over 'the evil eye'.

BASIL

Botanical name: *Ocicum basilicum*
Family: Lamiaceae (Labiatae)

For centuries basil has been appreciated in Europe and used for both culinary and medicinal purposes. It flourishes in the warmth of the Mediterranean countries where it is so successfully combined with sun-ripened tomatoes. The famous Pesto sauce originated in Genoa and it, perhaps more than anything else, is responsible for basil's return to favour in this country.

Basil was introduced to England in the sixteenth century and found its way to America in the seventeenth. In Stuart times it flavoured the famous Fetter Lane sausages, and it was also a custom of that time for farmers' wives to present pots of home-grown basil to their visitors. Like so many other herbs, its long period of subsequent neglect has only recently ended. Basil is easy and rewarding to grow but it needs a sunny, warm position in the garden and, unlike other labiate herbs, a rich well-fed soil. Seeds started indoors can be moved outside when all danger of frost is over. By pinching out any flower heads the plants will continue to produce fragrant and succulent leaves until early autumn. A good choice of seed varieties is available. Purple basil, bush basil with its tiny leaves, and the large-leaved lettuce basil all have excellent flavour. Basil does not dry well, but it can be preserved in jars – layer it with salt and cover with olive oil. Pesto can be frozen and is a delicious addition to soups or stews, and of course to pasta sauce.

BAY

Botanical name: *Laurus nobilis*
Family: Lauraceae

Bay is thought to originate in Asia Minor but it has been known in Mediterranean regions from pre-Christian times. Wreaths of bay leaves were used in early Greece and Rome to crown both poets and heroes, and bay is a potent symbol of wisdom in modern France as well. When my own daughter was seven, not so many years ago, she was crowned with a bay wreath for gaining top marks in school there, much to my delight. Bay is a surprisingly hardy tree and can be grown in tubs in southern England. Cuttings can be taken from half-ripe shoots in July.

Bay leaves can be used fresh but their aroma is improved when dried. They should be dried slowly in the dark then kept in air-tight jars. The leaves will vary in strength of flavour, depending on where they were grown and how long they have been dried, so use them carefully at first. They are an essential part of the bouquet garni and are used extensively to flavour stocks, stews, marinades and soups. Apart from savoury dishes they were also used in earlier centuries to flavour milk custards and puddings.

BERGAMOT

Botanical name: *Monarda didyma*
Family: Lamiaceae (Labiatae)

Bergamot is a perennial of the mint family and native to North America, where it is also known as Oswego tea after the Oswego Indians who used it. It can be grown from seed (sow in the shade) or by root division, but once established should be divided every three years as the central clumps tend to die back. Because bees are partial to its delicious fragrance it is sometimes known as bee balm. The many cultivated varieties have different coloured blossoms which can enhance both garden and salad bowl. Flowers from the red bergamot (*monarda didyma*) are particularly beautiful used with blue borage flowers. Young leaves can be used in salads and in sauces, particularly with pork.

BORAGE

Botanical name: *Borago officinalis*
Family: Boraginaceae

Borage is an easy annual to grow and a favourite with bees. Once established it will seed itself year after year. The leaves have a cucumber taste and can be chopped and added to salads when they are very young, and not too hairy. In Liguria, where borage grows in profusion, the leaves are used as a stuffing for ravioli. The charming blue flowers can decorate drinks, including Pimms No 1, and many different salads. Flowers frozen in ice cubes add charm to summer drinks and the flowers can also be crystallised and used for decorating cakes and puddings.

In 1629 John Parkinson described how borage was used 'in drinks that are cordiall, especially the flowers, which of Gentlewomen are candid for comffits'. John Evelyn in *Acetaria* (1699) writes of borage as being 'an exhilerating Cordial, of pleasant Flavour', and goes on to say that although the tender leaves 'and flowers especially' may be eaten in salads 'above all, the Sprigs in Wine, like those of Baum (lemon balm) are of known virtue to revive the Hypochondriac, and to chear the hard student'.

CHERVIL

Botanical name: *Anthriscus cerefolium*
Family: Umbelliferae

Chervil is a particularly delectable herb and the most delicate of the *fines herbes*. It has long been appreciated in France where its lovely delicate leaves and special anise flavour make it one of their most popular herbs. Happily, with the increased interest in herbs, it has become more available here. Easily grown in the garden it germinates quickly, but also is quick to go to seed so must be sown frequently. You can have chervil in your garden most of the winter if you sow in August and September. Pick the leaves from the outside to encourage centre growth. The flavour of chervil is evanescent when heated, so it is best added to hot dishes at the last moment. It is excellent in butters and delicious in salads and will provide fragrant but subtle sauces for both fish and fowl. It does not dry successfully.

CHIVE

Botanical name: *Allium schoenoprasum*
Family: Alliaceae

Chives are a hardy perennial that can be grown from seed but are more often propagated by dividing the clumps. The long, hollow, grass-like stems thrive on being cut and will grow again and again. It is a most useful herb to have at hand to add to omelettes, soups and salads or cream cheese. Its mild, onion flavour particularly enhances potatoes and tomatoes. The mauve flower can be eaten in salads or omelettes. Chives can also be used dried.

CORIANDER

Botanical name: *Coriandrum sativum*
Family: Apiaceae (Umbelliferae)

Coriander, one of the most ancient herbs, is native to Europe and the Middle East and was introduced to Britain by the Romans. The leaf has been used as a herb and the seed as a spice for hundreds of years throughout the Middle East, India, the Far East, Central and South America. Until recently only the seed has been in general use in this country but now, with growing interest in Eastern food, the leaves, which have a different flavour from the seeds, are more appreciated.

Coriander has a leaf very similar to the flat-leafed continental parsley and is usually available from Greek grocers in large bunches complete with roots. It is an annual and easy to grow from seed but in my experience, the home-grown variety produce more feathery and less aromatic leaves than the coriander which you can buy and which is normally imported. Because its flavour is assertive it should be used with a light hand. Try it with lentil or bean dishes or add a few chopped leaves to salads. The leaves do not dry well.

DILL

Botanical name: *Anethum graveolens*
Family: Apiaceae (Umbelliferae)

Dill is a most useful herb and happily one that is easy to grow if a sunny position can be found. It has feathery leaves very like fennel but is a much smaller plant with its own special flavour. Like coriander, its seeds are useful in cooking as a spice and its leaves (often called dill weed) as a herb and each has its own distinct taste. Dill is enormously popular in Central Europe where cucumbers are pickled in it and potatoes dressed with it. In Scandinavia it is the preferred herb with fish and the famous cured salmon – *gravad-lax* – bears its botanical

name. Dill is so versatile that in Turkey and Greece it flavours spinach, chicken and lamb dishes. It should be added to hot sauces at the last moment as its flavour is quick to fade on contact with heat. The most successful dried variety of the herb is freeze-dried.

ELDER

Botanical name: *Sambucus nigra*
Family: Caprifoliaceae

Elder is a very common small tree found in Europe, Asia and North America. Its tenacity and ability to spring up in unwanted places make it unpopular with today's gardener, but in previous centuries the elder was much appreciated. Needles, skewers, combs and toys were made from the close-grained wood. Infusions made from the leaves were spread on face and arms as an insect repellant and the leaves were scattered wherever grain was stored to discourage mice. The root, bark, leaves, berries and flowers have many medicinal uses, both real and imagined, from curing sciatic pains to removing freckles. The white blossom will flavour syrups and sorbets with its muscatel grape scent and can be added to stewed gooseberries or jelly. The berries can be stewed or used in chutneys. Home-made wine is still brewed today from the flowers and berries. Elderflower fritters are superb and freely available for anyone living near a park or in the country.

FENNEL

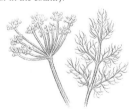

Botanical name: *Foeniculum vulgare*
Family: Apiaceae (Umbelliferae)

Fennel is a large hardy perennial that grows between three and five feet tall and has handsome feathery leaves. It grows wild in the temperate regions of Europe, particularly around the Mediterranean, and Romans were probably responsible for introducing it to Britain. Many varieties of fennel are grown for the seed which lends its distinctive anise flavour to liqueurs. The feathery leaves, chopped, are delicious in salads and sauces, particularly with fish. In France the dried stalks and flowers are burned on fires whose smoke then imparts a special taste to grilled fish. Florentine fennel is grown for its bulb which can be used as a raw or cooked vegetable.

LEMON BALM

Botanical name: *Melissa officinalis*
Family: Lamiaceae (Labiatae)

Lemon balm is an invasive, free-growing perennial which looks very like mint. It is not easy to buy bunches of this lemony herb but it is easy to grow either from seed or by root division. The charming generic name *Melissa*, which is the Greek for 'bee', derives from its use as a bee food. Bee keepers since the ancient Greeks have planted balm next to their hives, not only as a source of nectar but because, according to Pliny, it was thought that bees 'when they strayed away they do find their way home by it'. An eighteenth-century author suggests rubbing the inside of the bee hives with balm to stop the bees 'vagabonding'. As for its medicinal properties, John Evelyn wrote that 'Balm is sovereign for the brain, strengthening memory and powerfully chasing away melancholy'. The Elizabethans used it in tea and salads and as a flavouring for wine. Although the flavour is not as assertive as the smell, the leaves should be used sparingly, and always fresh not dried. Try adding a pinch of finely chopped balm to soups or salads. Or add a few sprigs to refresh summer drinks or white-wine cups. The Spanish make a milk drink with it – *leche perfumada con melisa*, and in France it is the basis for a liqueur – *eau-de-melisse des carmes*.

HYSSOP

Botanical name: *Hyssopus officinalis*
Family: Lamiaceae (Labiatae)

Another favourite with bees, hyssop is an attractive evergreen perennial spiked with blue and purple flowers. It comes from southern Europe and Russia and is a fairly hardy herb with a preference for calcareous soil. It looks something like savory and the two can be used interchangeably in recipes. Chopped young hyssop leaves, can flavour soup or sauces and mix well with cream or cottage cheese. Scattered in salads the flowers, as well as the young leaves, add a fresh peppery taste. Oil distilled from the leaves, stems and flowers has long been valued by perfumiers, and the medicinal uses of hyssop are legion. Planted near grapevines, it will supposedly increase their yield.

LOVAGE

Botanical name: *Levisticum officinale*
Family: Apiaceae (Umbelliferae)

Lovage can grow extremely tall and looks like a giant celery plant. Its strong flavour is also reminiscent of celery but is far more distinctive. The young leaves can be added to salads or soups, but should be used very sparingly. Mediterranean countries use the crushed seed to flavour bread and cakes. In earlier times the leaf stalks were blanched like celery and candied like angelica.

Lovage can be grown easily, but only from seeds that have recently ripened as they quickly lose their ability to germinate. (The same applies to angelica). It can also be propagated by division.

MARJORAM

Botanical names:
Origanum majorana (sweet or knotted marjoram)
Origanum vulgare (wild marjoram or oregano)
Origanum onites (pot marjoram)
Family: Labiatae

Wild marjoram grows in many parts of Europe, the Mediterranean and the British Isles. Its flavour varies enormously depending on the climate in which it is grown. The warmer climates produce very aromatic 'oregano' which is dried and used in tomato sauces, pizzas and with grilled meats. Sweet marjoram has a particularly good flavour and the leaves are best used fresh in salads, soups or sauces. Pot marjoram lacks this sweet flavour but is hardy and can be useful for more strongly flavoured dishes in combination with onion, wine and garlic. All marjorams, and there are many, are perennial but sweet marjoram is only half-hardy and must be treated as an annual.

MINT

Botanical name: species of *Mentha*
Family: Lamiaceae (Labiatae)
Most varieties of mint are vigorous perennials which spread rapidly by underground runners. For this reason they are best planted in a well contained area where they will have no chance of suffocating neighbouring plants. Mint thrives best in rich moist ground. Spearmint or applemint are most commonly used for mint sauce, jellies and as a flavouring for peas and new potatoes. Peppermint leaves produce a digestive tea. Young leaves from many mints, including the delicious pineapple and lemon mint, are excellent sprinkled sparingly in salads and added to cold or hot drinks. The tradition of serving mint with lamb is both old and sound; the natural oils in the mint counteract the fattiness of the lamb and make it more digestible. Mint is delicious in fruit salads and sorbets and the leaves can be crystallised for decorative purposes.

PARSLEY

Botanical name: *Petroselinum crispum*
Family: Apiaceae (Umbelliferae)
Parsley is a biennial but to ensure a constant supply it should be sown at least twice a year. The curly-leafed variety that is popular in this country is notoriously slow

to germinate. The flat-leafed 'continental' parsley comes up quickly and has excellent flavour. All parts of the plant can be used in cooking; don't neglect the root when the plant is in its second year and needs replacing. This well-known herb is crucial to many famous sauces such as ravigote, vinaigrette and sauce verte. It plays a vital role in the bouquet garni – the stems, which have more flavour are best here – and is the basis for the *fines herbes* mixture. Garlic and parsley are fine partners in persillade – a finely chopped mixture of the two, sautéed, and added at the last minute to stews and other dishes – and, of course, for stuffing snails.

PURSLANE

Botanical name: *Portulaca oleracea*
Family: Portulacaceae
Purslane is a succulent herb that was popular in the days of Elizabeth I. It is an annual well worth finding space for in the garden because the leaves are such a delicious addition to salads. There is a golden-leafed species which is particularly attractive and seeds for a winter variety can be purchased in France. The fleshy leaves with their subtle peppery taste enhance any salad and can also be used in soups in combination with sorrel or lettuce.

ROCKET

Botanical name: *Eruca sativa*
Family: Cruciferae
Rocket or rugola, as it is called in Italy, is another interesting salad herb that was known to the Romans and was in use in Elizabethan England. It has been popular in Italy and southern France for centuries and is finally coming back into favour in England and North America. In Italy today it is sold either in bunches on its own or with other salad greens. It has a special,

rather strong flavour that needs to be tempered by a vinaigrette dressing. It is very easy to grow from seed and comes up almost overnight, but needs to be sown at frequent intervals for a steady supply.

ROSEMARY

Botanical name: *Rosmarinus officinalis*
Family: Lamiaceae (Labiatae)
Despite its Mediterranean origins rosemary can enhance gardens in southern England if planted in a sunny sheltered position. It has charming blue flowers that blossom early and its evergreen spiky leaves can be used throughout the year for many culinary and other purposes.

Rosemary is for remembrance, Ophelia reminds us. The ancient Greeks believed this as well and students wove sprigs of rosemary in their hair to help their memory. Crush a few leaves in your hand, close your eyes and inhale the aroma – you can feel your head clear. A beneficial hair rinse can be made by simmering several branches in half a pint of water for thirty minutes.

Fresh rosemary branches are burned in fires to impart a subtle and delicious flavour to grilled meat. It is used extensively in marinades, and branches can also be placed under pork or lamb roasts while they cook. Because the leaves are spiky and strong flavoured they should be carefully removed before serving. The tender young leaves, very finely chopped and in very tiny amounts, can flavour sauces for duck or game.

SAGE

Botanical name: *Salvia officinalis*
Family: Lamiaceae (Labiatae)
Sage was used medicinally by the Romans and held in high esteem for its healthful properties throughout the ages. Nicholas Culpeper, who was well aware of its antiseptic qualities, wrote in 1653 'Gargles likewise are made with Sage . . . with some Honey put thereto to wash sore Mouthes and Throats'. Perhaps it is

frequently included in stuffings for goose and other fatty meats because it is known to aid digestion. The Italians are fond of sage with liver and veal, as a stuffing for ravioli, and for wrapping small game birds before roasting. It can be used dried but the flavour is far less agreeable.

SAVORY

Botanical names:
Satureja hortensis (summer savory)
Satureja montana (winter savory)
Family: Labiatae
There are many varieties of savory but the most commonly used in cooking are summer and winter savory. Summer savory is an annual and winter savory a perennial that will keep its leaves in mild winters. The latter also grows into a bushy shrub and can be used to border herb gardens. The flavours of the two are similar but summer savory has the more gentle flavour. In Provence where winter savory is known as *poivre d'ane* (donkey pepper) it is used to wrap around creamy goats cheese, in rabbit stews and with lentils. Like thyme, which it can replace in the kitchen, savory can be used dried. Rubbing the leaves from either of the two savories on a bee sting will give quick relief.

SORREL

Botanical names:
Rumex acetosa (common sorrel)
Rumex rugosus Campdera (garden sorrel)
Rumex scutatus (French sorrel)
Family: Polygonaceae
Sorrel was used by the Romans and has been a popular herb in European countries, especially France, for centuries. All the cultivated sorrels derive from the wild species. Garden and French sorrel are the two most popular varieties and both are easy to grow. It is very

hard to buy sorrel at the greengrocers but if you can find room in your garden for just a few plants you will have enough sorrel leaves to make delicious lemony-flavoured sauces. When using sorrel pull out the centre stalks and discard them before chopping the leaves. The leaves will quickly dissolve into the sauce or soup and so should be added at the last minute. A few tender young leaves, devoid of stalks, rolled up like cigars and sliced to make a chiffonade are a delicious addition to salads.

TARRAGON

Botanical name: *Artemesia dracunculus*
Family: Compositae

Tarragon must hold top place in any cook's list of favourite herbs. Its wonderful flavour adds a magical touch to sauces for fish, fowl, eggs and many vegetables. It is famous as a flavouring for vinegar – a recipe is included. Enliven your salads by shredding a few fresh leaves into them, or mix some chopped leaves into the vinaigrette. French tarragon has the best flavour and is grown from cuttings and root division. When buying a tarragon plant, even one labeled French tarragon, it is prudent to pinch a leaf and sniff it to find out if the aroma is sufficiently strong. The plants should be renewed every four or five years because they tend to lose flavour with age. Freeze-dried tarragon is the best of the dried varieties but not a patch on the fresh, which happily is becoming more and more available.

THYME

Botanical name: *Thymus vulgaris*
Family: Lamiaceae (Labiatae)

Thyme is a well known and important culinary herb. It originated in southern Europe and the Mediterranean where it still perfumes the sunny dry landscape. There are many cultivated varieties that grow well in Britain provided they have sun and well-drained soil. Upright varieties make lovely low borders and creeping thymes add charm to rock gardens. Thyme also does well in window boxes and needs little attention. Some species of thyme are more aromatic than others. Garden thyme and lemon thyme are among the best and are very useful in the kitchen but they cannot rival the fragrance of their wild Mediterranean cousin. In Greece it is used fresh in salads and to flavour lamb. It is also wonderful in marinades and is part of the bouquet garni. Thyme is an evergreen perennial and can be used fresh or dried – it is, in fact, one of the few herbs that improves with drying.

RECIPES

SOUPS

CARROT, ORANGE AND MINT SOUP   *Serves 4*

1 large onion, chopped
500g (1lb) carrots, chopped
25g (1oz/2 tbsp) butter
900ml (1½pt/4 cups) chicken stock
grated rind and juice of one large orange
4 tbsp of finely chopped mint leaves
150ml (¼pt/⅔ cup) single cream
salt and freshly ground black pepper

Sauté the onion in the butter over gentle heat until the onion softens. Add the carrots and stir until they are coated in the butter. Add the stock, cover, and simmer until the carrots are soft. Add 3 tbsp of the mint, and the rind and juice of the orange, cover, and leave to infuse for 15 minutes before whizzing up in a blender or processor. Season with salt and pepper. Before serving reheat with the cream to just below a boil. Serve garnished with the reserved mint.

SORREL AND LENTIL SOUP   *Serves 6-8*

350g (12oz) green or brown lentils
1 large onion, chopped
1½l (2½pt) chicken stock
bouquet garni
250g (8oz) sorrel
150ml (¼pt/⅔ cup) smetana or soured cream
salt and freshly ground black pepper

Pick over the lentils for any stones and wash. Place lentils, onion, stock and bouquet garni in a large saucepan. Cover and simmer for at least 1¼ hours or until lentils are very soft. Check during cooking to see if more stock or water needs to be added.

Meanwhile wash the sorrel, pull off the stalks and discard. Set aside a few leaves for the garnish. Shred the rest of the sorrel coarsely. When the lentils are soft add the sorrel and cook uncovered for a minute or two – just to wilt the leaves. Purée the soup in a blender or processor and sieve the purée if you want a finer consistency. Season and keep refrigerated until needed. Before serving reheat to just below the boil, stir in the smetana or soured cream and serve garnished with a few strands of sorrel.

CORIANDER SOUP
Serves 8

This soup is particularly good cold and will provide a different and exotic start for a summer meal.

1 medium-sized onion, very finely chopped
25g (1oz/2 tbsp) butter
175g (6oz) courgettes (zucchini), peeled and chopped
75g (3oz/1 cup) fresh coriander (cilantro) leaves, chopped
salt and freshly ground black pepper
3 tbsp semolina
900ml (1½ pt/4 cups) chicken stock
If serving hot
110ml (4floz/½ cup) whipping cream
2 egg yolks
If serving cold
250g (9oz) tub thick-set Greek yoghurt
Garnish
Fresh coriander leaves, finely chopped and toasted slivered almonds

Sweat the onion in the butter until soft without allowing it to colour. Add the courgettes and coriander, and stir for a few minutes. Add 900ml (1½ pt/3 cups) of salted water and bring to the boil. Stir in the semolina. Cover and simmer for 20 minutes or until the courgettes are tender. Purée in a blender or processor. Thin by adding the stock.

To serve hot Reheat the soup to just below a simmer. Whisk cream and egg yolks together. Stir in two ladles of hot soup, then pour back into the soup and heat gently without allowing it to come near the boil. Garnish and serve.

To serve cold Stir in the yoghurt, taste for seasoning and garnish with coriander and almonds.

CREAM OF FENNEL AND MUSSEL SOUP *Serves 4*

1kg (2lb) mussels
2 shallots, chopped finely
2 tbsp parsley, chopped finely
glass of dry white wine, plus 1 tbsp
13g (½oz/1 tbsp) butter
1 tbsp oil
½ small carrot, chopped finely
¼ stalk of celery, chopped finely
1 bulb of fennel
300ml (½pt/1¼ cups) fish or chicken stock
small pinch of saffron

Cream of fennel and mussel soup

17

1 tsp Pernod
5 tbsp cream
1 egg yolk
salt and freshly ground black pepper

Scrub the mussels, then place them in a bowl of cold salted water. Discard any that are open. Place half the shallots, half the parsley and the glass of wine in a large saucepan. Bring to the boil and add the mussels. Cover the pan and cook over brisk heat for about 5 minutes – just long enough for the mussels to open. Overcooking will toughen them. Strain over a bowl. Remove the mussels from their shells and strain the broth through a muslin lined sieve. Place the saffron in 1 tbsp of wine and leave to infuse. Using a small heavy-bottomed saucepan sweat the remaining shallot, parsley, carrot and celery in the butter and oil until soft. Remove any coarse outer stalks from the fennel and discard. Finely slice the rest and add to the pan. Stir for a few minutes and season with salt and pepper. Add a ladle of the stock, cover, and simmer very gently until tender. Stir in the Pernod then turn the mixture into a blender and purée, adding more stock as necessary. Pour into a clean saucepan, add the mussel broth, saffron and 4 tbsp of the cream. Adjust the seasoning. Before serving reheat the soup, mix the egg yolk with the remaining cream and stir into the soup. Add the mussels and heat to just below the boil.

CUCUMBER AND DILL SOUP   *Serves 8*
Delicious cold as well as hot.

1 large onion, finely chopped
2 cucumbers
25g (1oz/2 tbsp) butter
1⅓l (2 pt/5 cups) chicken stock
2 tbsp tarragon vinegar
5 tbsp semolina (or quick cooking farina)
50g (2oz/⅓ cup) fresh dill weed, finely chopped
175ml (6floz/¾ cup) single (light) cream
salt and freshly ground black pepper

Using a large heavy-bottomed saucepan sweat the onion in the butter until soft. Peel the cucumbers, slice and stir into the onions. Add the vinegar and stock and bring to the boil. Once the mixture has boiled stir in the semolina. Season well, cover, and simmer for about 25 minutes or until the cucumber is very soft. Remove from the heat and leave until lukewarm. Blend with the dill and cream. Serve cold, or if serving hot heat to just below the boil.

FRESH TOMATO AND BASIL SOUP   *Serves 4-5*

A soup to make in the summer or whenever you have good-flavoured tomatoes and fresh basil at hand.

3 shallots
40g (1½oz) butter
1¼ kg (2½lb) tomatoes, seeded and chopped
300ml (½ pt/1¼ cups) chicken stock
10 basil leaves, shredded by hand
6 tbsp double cream
1 egg yolk
1 tsp sugar (optional)
salt and freshly ground black pepper

Gently sweat the shallots in the butter until tender without colouring butter or shallots. Stir in the tomatoes and half the basil and simmer, covered, for 5 minutes. Add the stock and cook a further 5 minutes. Sieve through the finest disc of a vegetable mill or purée and work through a sieve. Whisk the cream, egg yolk and remaining basil together in a small bowl. Reheat the soup to just below the boil, ladle some soup on to the egg mixture while whisking then return the mixture to the pan and heat a minute more. Do not allow it to come near the boil. Taste and adjust the seasoning adding the sugar if necessary. Serve immediately. The soup can be prepared ahead, up to adding the cream and egg enrichment.

LEEK, CARROT AND TARRAGON SOUP *Serves 4*

1 tbsp olive oil
6 carrots, sliced
1 medium-sized onion, chopped
2 leeks, green and white parts, sliced
1 stalk celery, sliced
300ml (½pt/1¼ cups) chicken stock
2 tsp chopped fresh tarragon
6 tbsp milk
salt and freshly ground black pepper

Heat the olive oil in a saucepan, add the vegetables, and stir until they are coated in the oil. Add the stock and enough water to cover the vegetables. Simmer, covered, until they are tender. Drop the tarragon into a blender and add a small ladle of the hot soup. Blend for a few seconds, add the rest of the soup and purée. Return the mixture to the saucepan, rinse out the blender with the milk and add to the pan. Season with salt and pepper and more tarragon if necessary.

Nettle Soup
Serves 4

The time to make this soup is early spring when the nettles are just starting to shoot up. Wear gloves and only pick the bright green tops and young leaves. The formic acid responsible for the sting is destroyed when the nettles are cooked and you will end up with a soup tasting much like spinach.

50g (2oz/4 tbsp) butter
1 medium-sized onion, chopped
450g (1lb) young nettle shoots
2 cloves of garlic, chopped
3 medium-size potatoes, peeled and diced
1l (1¾pt/4¼ cups) light chicken stock or water
salt and freshly ground black pepper
300ml (½pt/1¼ cups) whipping cream
few gratings of nutmeg

Soften the onion in the butter without allowing it to colour. Wash the nettles and chop coarsely. Stir them into the soup along with the garlic. Add the potatoes and coat them in the butter before adding the stock and seasoning. Simmer, covered, until the vegetables are tender. Sieve the soup through the finest disc of a vegetable mill. Before serving heat with the cream to just below boiling point, season with nutmeg and serve.

FIRST COURSES

TARRAGON PEARS WITH HAM   *Serves 8*

This is a variation of Parma ham and pear, a combination that is popular in
Italy. The tarragon sauce adds an extra dimension.

1 egg
2 tbsp caster sugar
3 tbsp tarragon vinegar
450ml (¾pt/1½ cups) double cream, whipped
16 slices of Parma ham, paper thin
4 ripe pears, preferably passa crassana or comice
50g (2oz) walnuts, chopped
chopped fresh tarragon for the garnish

Whisk the egg, sugar and vinegar together in a bain-marie over barely
simmering water until the mixture thickens. Whisk off heat until cool.
Whip the cream and fold into the egg mixture. Refrigerate covered if not
using immediately. Peel, halve and core the pears. Place 2 slices of ham on
individual plates. Set a half pear on the ham and coat with the sauce.
Sprinkle with walnuts and fresh tarragon.

STUFFED VINE LEAVES (*Dolmathes*) *Makes about 40*

These vine leaves stuffed with mint and rice are popular in Greece and can
be used as an *hors d'oeuvre* or as part of a mixed buffet. Rice is an excellent
base for the stuffing but other herbs can be used and cold cooked meats such
as lamb or chicken added.

For the stuffing
4 tbsp good olive oil
2 medium-sized onions, finely chopped
225g (8oz) rice
300ml (½pt/1¼ cups) boiling water
2 tbsp pine-nuts
1 tbsp currants
2 tbsp finely chopped fresh mint
1 tsp finely chopped fresh sage
1 tsp sugar
salt and freshly ground black pepper

For the Dolmathes
*4 dozen vine leaves, fresh or vacuum
   packed in brine*
600ml (1pt) water
juice of ½ lemon

Sauté the onion in the oil until soft, stir in the rice and coat in the oil, then
add the pine-nuts, currants, half the mint and the sage. Stir in the boiling

water, cover the pan, and simmer gently until the rice is cooked and the water absorbed. Turn into a shallow bowl and season with the sugar, salt and pepper and the remaining mint.

If using fresh vine leaves blanch in boiling water for a few minutes. If using vine leaves packed in brine pour boiling water over them and leave for 15 minutes. Rinse and drain.

Place a teaspoon of the stuffing on the underside of a leaf, roll up, tucking in the ends. Place in a baking dish lined with any torn leaves. Pack them tightly in the dish, add the water and lemon juice and cover. Bake in a low oven at about 170°C/325F/Gas Mark 3 for an hour. Leave them in the dish until cool then remove to a plate and keep in a cool place until serving.

Pesto Aubergine
Serves 6

Aubergines absorb a great deal of fat when they are fried in a small amount of oil but when they are deep fried in very hot fat they absorb very little. They can be prepared ahead and reheated under a hot grill or in a hot oven just before serving.

corn or groundnut oil
3 small firm aubergines
6 tbsp freshly grated Parmesan cheese
4-5 tbsp pesto (page 73)

Heat enough oil for deep frying to a temperature of about 185C (360F). Cut the aubergine in half lengthwise and fry one or two halves at a time. They should take about 7-8 minutes. Turn them over half way through the cooking time. Drain on paper towels. Heat an oven or grill until very hot. Slash the cut sides of the aubergine in a few places and smear with a mixture of pesto and cheese. Grill or bake to reheat before serving.

Potted Shrimps with Mint
Serves 6

An easy first course when made with frozen shrimps or prawns. It will keep for up to 2 weeks if kept refrigerated. Serve with hot toast.

250g (8oz/16 tbsp) butter
1 tsp mace
1 tbsp fresh mint, very finely chopped
salt and freshly ground black pepper
cayenne pepper
500g (1lb) shelled shrimps or prawns or crab or lobster, thawed if frozen

Gently heat 175g (6oz) of the butter, then add the mace, mint, some freshly ground black pepper and a pinch of cayenne. When the butter has melted stir in the shrimps. Heat until the shrimps are hot, taste for seasoning adding salt if necessary, then pour into a ceramic or glass jar or pot. Heat the remaining butter until just melted and pour over the shrimps to form a thin layer. The shrimps should be completely covered with butter. Refrigerate for at least 24 hours before using.

CALABRESE CREAM WITH LEMON THYME SAUCE

Serves 4

This creamy calabrese mousse served with a lemon thyme sauce makes a delicious and attractive first course.

For the custard
250g (8oz) calabrese with thin stalks
3oz (75g) boneless chicken breast
1 egg
1/4pt (150ml) double cream
4 tbsp milk
salt and pepper

For the sauce
1 tbsp butter
1 shallot, chopped very fine
6 tbsp dry white wine

150ml (1/4pt/⅝cup) very good chicken stock
1 tsp chopped, fresh lemon thyme leaves or half quantity dried
squeeze of lemon juice
2 tbsp cream
1 tsp arrowroot (optional)
salt and freshly ground black pepper

Peel the stalks of the calabrese. Cook both heads and stalks in a large quantity of boiling salted water, uncovered (so they retain their colour) until just tender, about 5 minutes. Drain and chop coarsely. Place the container of the food processor in the refrigerator to chill. Chop the cold chicken breast and process for a few minutes, until the chicken becomes a smooth paste. Add the cream and process again until smooth, then add the calabrese, egg and milk and process until well blended. Work the mixture through a fine sieve. Season well and divide between four small greased ramekins. Cover each ramekin tightly will foil, then make a few small slashes with a sharp knife over the top. Set the ramekins in a roasting pan lined with several layers of newspaper. Fill with hot water to come half-way up the sides of the dishes. Bake for 20-25 minutes in an oven preheated to 170°C/325°F/Gas Mark 3. Remove from the oven and roasting tin and let stand for a few minutes before turning out.

Meanwhile make the sauce by sweating the shallots and thyme in the butter until soft. Add the wine and reduce by half, then add the stock and reduce slightly. Stir in the cream and season to taste with salt and pepper and a squeeze of lemon juice. If you want a thicker sauce slake a teaspoon of arrowroot in a tablespoon of cold water, add to the sauce and simmer for a minute or two. Serve some sauce around each mousse.

Calabrese cream with lemon thyme sauce

Smoked mackerel and dill ravioli

Prawn and Mint Ravioli
Serves 8

This delicious ravioli really needs no sauce but if you feel it would look too bare try the red pepper sauce in Sam's Spanish Stuffed Peppers (page 27).

500g (1lb) prawns, defrosted if frozen
6 tbsp fromage frais 8% fat
3 tbsp finely shredded mint
salt and freshly ground pepper
64 won ton wrappers
egg yolk mixed with a little water

Chop the prawns and mix with the fromage frais, mint, salt and pepper. Prepare the ravioli and cook them following the instructions in Smoked Mackerel and Dill Ravioli. Serve on their own or with a red pepper sauce lightened with a bit of cream.

Smoked Mackerel and Dill Ravioli
Serves 4-5

Won Ton wrappers available in Oriental food stores are ideal for ravioli. They are easy to use and cook beautifully being both tender and strong. It makes a very special first course that belies the effort involved.

250g (8oz) skinned smoked mackerel fillets
6 tbsp fresh dill weed, chopped very fine
juice of half a lemon
freshly ground black pepper
175g (6oz) fresh ricotta cheese
6 tbsp cream
48 won ton wrappers
yolk of one egg mixed with a little water
1 tbsp oil
50g (2oz/4tbsp) butter

Mash the mackerel and all but a teaspoon of the dill together. Add lots of black pepper, the lemon juice, the ricotta and cream. Place a teaspoon of the mixture in the centre of a won ton square. Brush the egg wash around the edge and place another wrapper over the top pressing around the edge to seal. Cut into rounds with a pastry cutter. Continue until all the filling is used. Bring a large quantity of water to the boil, add 3 tbsp of salt and the oil. Slide the ravioli into the water, bring it back to the boil before lowering the heat to a gentle boil. Cook for about 2-3 minutes. Use a large Chinese flat sieve to remove them from the water or drain carefully over a colander. Heat the butter in a saucepan. Divide the ravioli between 4 heated plates and pour over the butter. Garnish with the reserved dill.

RICOTTA AND BASIL RAVIOLI

Serves 5-6

350g (12oz) ricotta cheese
24 basil leaves, chopped
25g (1oz) freshly grated Parmesan cheese, plus extra for serving
1 egg yolk
salt and freshly ground black pepper
64 won ton wrappers
yolk of one egg mixed with a little water
300ml (½pt/1¼ cups) tomato sauce (page 74)

Mix the ricotta, basil, Parmesan and one egg yolk together. Season to taste with salt and pepper. Follow the instructions for the Smoked Mackerel and Dill Ravioli for making and cooking these ravioli. Serve with the hot tomato sauce and extra Parmesan cheese if desired.

SAM'S SPANISH STUFFED PEPPER

Serves 6

This slice of red pepper filled with a creamy mixture of potato and smoked fish, served with a red pepper sauce makes a delicious first course. It also makes an excellent main dish but you will need to count on 1½ peppers per person, one to stuff and ½ for the sauce, and increase the other ingredients proportionately. Sam, a young chef, tasted a similar dish in Spain and devised this recipe on returning home.

4 red peppers
5 tbsp olive oil
1 tbsp sunflower oil
squeeze of lemon
salt and freshly ground black pepper
8 tbsp chives, chopped very fine
400g (14oz) smoked haddock
400g (14oz) peeled potatoes
300ml (½pt/1¼ cups) milk

Cut the stalks from the peppers and remove the core and seeds. Divide each pepper into 3 equal strips unless you are serving whole peppers as a main course. Place under a very hot grill skin side up, and grill until almost completely charred and black. Peel off the skin with wet fingers. Place in a shallow dish with 4 tbsp of the olive oil and leave overnight. Boil the potatoes and strain. Poach the fish in the milk and strain reserving the milk. Sieve both potatoes and fish through a vegetable mill into a bowl. Add just enough of the milk to make a soft mixture. Season with 6 tbsp of the chives and lots of black pepper. Taste before adding any salt – it may not need it. Divide the mixture between 6 pepper slices. Place them stuffing

Sam's Spanish stuffed pepper

Tuna and coriander pâté

side down on a lightly oiled baking tray and bake in a hot oven for 15 minutes or until well heated.

Meanwhile purée the remaining pepper slices in a blender with a squeeze of lemon, the sunflower oil and just enough olive oil to make a thin sauce. Heat in a small saucepan with the remaining chives and black pepper. Spoon some sauce on 6 dishes and place a pepper, red side up in the middle of each. Serve immediately. Both sauce and stuffed peppers can be prepared 2 days ahead if kept refrigerated.

TUNA AND CORIANDER PÂTÉ *Serves 8 as a first course*

For the pâté
2 small potatoes
2 x 200g (7oz) cans of tuna fish, packed in oil
4 tbsp freshly grated Parmesan cheese
2 tbsp fresh finely chopped coriander leaves
2 tbsp cream
squeeze of lemon juice
2 small eggs
salt and freshly ground black pepper

For the poaching liquid
1 stalk of celery
1 carrot
1 onion, sliced
2 bay leaves
a few sprigs of parsley

For the sauce
225ml (8floz/1 cup) thick set yoghurt
1 tsp finely chopped fresh mint
salt and pepper

Peel the potatoes and boil them in salted water until just tender. Drain then sieve them through a vegetable mill. Drain most of the oil from the tuna and discard. Mash the tuna with the cheese, coriander, cream, and eggs. Stir in the potato and season with the lemon juice, pepper and salt if necessary. Moisten a piece of muslin, wring dry, and lay it on a flat surface. Make a sausage shape, about 6.5 cm (2½ in) in diameter, with the tuna mixture and roll up in the cloth like a salami. Tie both ends with string. Using a saucepan large enough to contain the tuna roll, add the poaching ingredients and fill with enough water to cover the roll. Bring to a boil, add some salt and simmer very gently for 40 minutes. Remove from the liquid and when cool enough to handle remove the muslin. When cold slice carefully with a sharp serrated knife and serve with a bowl of yoghurt flavoured with mint, salt and pepper.

TROUT AND SOLE SEVICHE *Serves 6*

Any fresh fish can be used for seviche, but this combination of pink trout and sole makes a very attractive first course. For a light lunch it could be served in half an avocado.

450g (1lb) trout fillets, skinned
450g (1lb) sole fillets, skinned

150ml (¼ pt/²⁄₃ cup) lime juice
½ red onion or 6 spring onions, sliced very fine
1 tsp freshly ground black pepper
½ cup of finely chopped fresh coriander leaves
2 tbsp olive oil
1½ tsp salt
3 medium tomatoes, skinned, seeded and chopped
1 tbsp very finely chopped parsley
lettuce

Remove any bones from the fillets with tweezers then cut into thin slices. Mix with the lime juice, spring onions, pepper, coriander, oil and salt. Cover and refrigerate for at least 3 hours. Mix with the chopped tomatoes and serve in a heap on lettuce leaves garnished with fresh parsley.

CURED FISH WITH HERBS
Serves 6

There are endless recipes for *gravad-lax* – cured salmon – but very few for cheaper fish such as mackerel. The method is the same whatever fish you use and a combination of fish makes a more interesting looking and tasting dish. Dill is the most common choice for a herb and is particularly good with salmon, but coriander and basil are delicious too. Except for freeze-dried dill, fresh herbs are a must. Once cured the fish freeze beautifully and can be cut paper thin before completely thawed.

3 good-sized very fresh mackerel,
   filleted but not skinned
25g (1oz) sea salt
20g (¾oz/2 tbsp) sugar
good bunch of coriander or dill or basil,
   roughly chopped

For the sauce
4 tbsp Dijon mustard

2 tsp caster sugar
3 tbsp mild wine vinegar
1 tsp salt
150ml (¼pt/½ cup) groundnut
   or sunflower oil
2-3 tbsp of the same fresh herb used
   to cure the fish, chopped

Remove any bones from the fillets with tweezers. Mix the salt and sugar together. Place the fillets skin down and rub the cut side with the mixture. Sprinkle with some of the herb. Sandwich the fish back together and sprinkle the skins with the rest of the herb. Wrap each fish in cling-film, then place in one layer in a dish. Place a board, then a 1.4 kg (3 lb) weight on top. Refrigerate for 1-3 days.

Unwrap the fish, drain off the liquid and pat dry. Wrap in fresh cling-film and place in the freezer for a few hours to facilitate slicing. Cut into very thin diagonal slices.

Stir the first 4 sauce ingredients together and gradually whisk in the oil as for a mayonnaise. Stir in the herb and serve with the sliced fish.

TARRAGON AND CIDER SORBET *Serves 8*

150ml (¼pt/⅔ cup) water
50g (2oz/¼ cup) sugar
8-10 good sprigs of tarragon
600ml (1 pt) dry French sparkling cider, chilled

Dissolve the sugar in the water and bring to a boil. Add the tarragon and simmer for 5 minutes then turn off the heat, cover, and leave to infuse. When the syrup has a strong tarragon flavour strain it and leave to cool. The strength of tarragon varies so you may have to add more tarragon and simmer again if the flavour seems weak. Mix the cool syrup with the cider and freeze in the usual way.

DILL AND VODKA SORBET *Serves 6*

124g (4oz) fresh dill weed, chopped
100g (3½oz) caster sugar
salt and a few black peppercorns
lemon juice
shot of vodka

Bring 900 ml (1½ pt) of water with the sugar to a boil; add the dill, a pinch of salt and the peppercorns. When the mixture returns to a rolling boil turn off the heat, cover, and leave to infuse for 5 minutes. Pour into a bowl and leave to cool. Purée in a blender then press through a fine sieve. Season with salt, lemon juice and the vodka. Freeze in the usual way. Because of the low sugar content the sorbet will become very hard and turn to ice if left too long. Either use it several hours after it has been churned, or if it does go hard cut into chunks and process it before serving.

TOMATO AND BASIL SORBET *Serves 8*

A very refreshing sorbet that could be served with a few spoonfuls of vodka as an alternative to a Bloody Mary.

900g (2lb) ripe tomatoes
2 shallots, chopped very fine
3 tsp of sugar
handful of fresh basil leaves, very finely chopped
squeeze of lemon juice
dash of tobasco
salt and pepper

Chop the tomatoes and put half into a saucepan with the shallots, sugar and some salt and pepper. Gently simmer, covered, for about 10 minutes. Pour the cooked tomatoes into a blender, purée, then sieve back into the saucepan. Add the chopped basil, cover the pan, and leave to infuse. Meanwhile whizz the other half of the tomatoes in a blender and sieve into a bowl. When the cooked tomatoes have cooled combine them with the uncooked purée and season with tobasco, lemon juice, and salt and pepper if needed. Freeze in the ordinary way. If the sorbet has been frozen in a freezer instead of an ice cream machine you may want to break it up into chunks and whizz it for a minute in a food processor to soften before serving.

TARRAGON BAKED EGGS
Serves 1

butter for greasing
2 tbsp double cream
1 tsp chopped fresh tarragon leaves
1 fresh free range egg
salt and pepper

Preheat the oven to 190°C/375°F/Gas Mark 6. Grease a ramekin with butter. Add 1 tbsp of the cream and sprinkle half the herbs in the ramekin. Set the ramekin in a roasting tin and pour boiling water into the tin to come half way up the side of the ramekin. Set over moderate heat until the cream is hot. Carefully break an egg into the ramekin, season with salt and pepper and cover with the remaining cream and herbs. Set the tin in the oven and bake for about 7 minutes or until the yolk is just set. The egg should tremble when it is moved. The egg can be left in the water bath out of the oven for 10 minutes before serving. If you are cooking several eggs place a few layers of newspaper on the bottom of the roasting tin before adding the ramekins and hot water. This will prevent them slipping about.

LIGHT MEALS

BUCKWHEAT CRÊPES WITH TOMATO, MOZZARELLA AND BASIL
Serves 8

These buckwheat crêpes from Normandy combine beautifully with the Italian flavours of mozzarella, tomato and basil. The crêpe recipe will make about 14 crêpes. Use all the batter and freeze any extra crêpes. One of these filled crêpes will make a light lunch served perhaps with a salad.

For the crêpes
75g (3oz) buckwheat flour
25g (1oz) plain flour
50g (2oz/5 tbsp) butter, plus extra for greasing
3 eggs
300ml (½pt/1¼ cups) milk

For the filling
12 tomatoes, skinned, seeded and chopped roughly
600g (1¼lb) mozzarella cheese
1½ tbsp virgin extra olive oil
30 basil leaves, finely shredded
salt and freshly ground black pepper

Sift both flours into a bowl. Make a well in the centre and break in the eggs. Melt the butter very gently with some of the milk. Add the rest of the milk then stir gradually into the flour mixture. Season with salt. Leave to rest for 15 minutes. Heat a 24cm (9½in) cast-iron frying pan. Rub the pan with buttered paper and pour in a small ladle of the crêpe mixture. Tilt the pan so the bottom is evenly and quickly coated. Pour out any excess and use less batter the next time. Cook over high heat for about 1 minute, flip over and cook the second side for a shorter time. Add a little water to the batter if the consistency of the crêpe is too thick. It will take a few crêpes before the consistency, amount of batter and heat are just right. Pile them on a plate and when cool layer with greaseproof paper if you are not stuffing immediately.

Heat the tomatoes very gently in the olive oil to just warm through, add the diced mozzarella and stir a few minutes longer then take off the heat and stir in the basil. Season with salt and pepper. Strain the tomato mixture over a bowl. Divide the mixture between 8 crêpes rolling them up in turn and placing in a shallow oven dish. Pour the strained juices over the crêpes and bake in a very hot oven for about 10 minutes before serving.

Buckwheat Crêpes with Courgette and Tarragon
Serves 8

Make the crêpes following the recipe for Buckwheat Crêpes with Tomato, Mozzarella and Basil.

1.5kg (3½lb) small firm courgettes (zucchini)
salt and pepper
2 medium-sized red onions, chopped finely
50g (2oz/4 tbsp) butter
125ml (4floz/½ cup) double cream
3 tsp fresh tarragon, chopped

Peel some of the skin from the courgettes before grating them coarsely. Sprinkle with salt and leave for 20 minutes. Rinse then squeeze the grated courgettes by the handful to extract some of the moisture. Soften the onion in the butter in a frying pan. Add the cream and tarragon and stir for one minute before adding the courgettes. Raise the heat and stir for several minutes, until the courgettes are tender. Season with pepper and salt if needed. Fill and bake as above. The crêpes will be crisp and the filling creamy.

Omelette Fines Herbes
Serves 2

It is crucial to have the right sized pan for omelettes. A heavy-based iron or aluminium pan 23cm (9in) in diameter is perfect for a 4-5 egg omelette for two – 17cm (7in) diameter pans will make a 2-3 egg omelette for one person.

4-5 very fresh free-range eggs
salt and freshly ground black pepper
2 tbsp butter
2 tsp each of chopped fresh parsley, chervil and chives
1 tsp chopped fresh tarragon

Beat the eggs with salt and pepper in a bowl until whites and yolk are just combined. Melt the butter in the pan over medium-heat until it foams and is just beginning to brown. Pour in the eggs and stir them quickly with the flat end of a fork for a few seconds. Lift the egg that is starting to cook around the edge of the pan, tilting the pan at the same time so the uncooked egg runs to the sides. Sprinkle the herbs over the omelette and when it is mostly set, but still a bit runny, fold it by tipping the pan away from you. With the help of a fork fold the near edge of the omelette into the omelette's centre. Fold the far edge toward the centre and half roll and slide the omelette on to a warmed serving dish.

Buckwheat crêpes with tomato, mozzarella and basil

Omelette fines herbes

SORREL OMELETTE

Replace the herbs with a few tablespoons of finely shredded young sorrel leaves that have had their centre stalks removed.

CHIVE OR MARJORAM FLOWER OMELETTE

Add several chive or marjoram blossoms to the omelette in place of the herbs.

SCRAMBLED EGGS WITH TOMATO AND BASIL
Serves 4

4 tomatoes, peeled, seeded and chopped
2 cloves garlic, crushed
good pinch of sugar
bouquet garni
3 tbsp virgin extra olive oil
50g (2oz/4 tbsp) butter
10 eggs, lightly beaten and seasoned
salt and pepper
15-20 fresh basil leaves
4 pieces of toasted buttered bread

Heat the olive oil in a small frying pan, add the tomatoes, garlic, sugar, salt and pepper and bouquet garni. Stir until the juices from the tomatoes have evaporated and the mixture separates. Discard the garlic and bouquet garni. Add the butter and eggs to the pan, and stir over gentle heat until the mixture thickens. Stir in the basil and taste for seasoning. Serve on toasted, buttered bread.

LOVAGE SOUFFLÉ
Serves 4-5

A soufflé is one of the best ways I have found for using this very intriguing but easily overpowering herb. Individual soufflé dishes are a very attractive and easy way to cope with dinner party soufflés.

45g (1½oz/4 tbsp) butter, plus extra for greasing
30g (1 oz/3 tbsp) flour
300ml (½pt/1¼ cups) milk
half bay leaf
4 egg yolks
2 tbsp freshly grated Parmesan cheese
5 or 6 egg whites
2 tsp fresh lovage leaves, chopped
salt and freshly ground black pepper

Melt the butter in a small saucepan, whisk in the flour and when the mixture is smooth pour the milk and bay leaf into the pan. Whisk until the mixture is fairly thick. Remove the pan from the heat and stir in the egg yolks, one at a time, then add the cheese. Season to taste and add the lovage. Whisk the egg whites with a pinch of salt until stiff then fold into the yolk mixture. Grease either a 1¼l (2½pt) soufflé dish or 4-5 300 ml (½pt) dishes. Bake in an oven preheated to 200°C/400°F/Gas Mark 6. Allow 20-25 minutes for one large soufflé and 12 minutes for small ones. Serve immediately. Soufflés can be prepared ahead up to whisking the egg whites. Reheat the yolk mixture slightly before folding in the whites and cooking the soufflés.

PESTO SOUFFLÉ Serves 4-5

Follow the recipe for Lovage Soufflé omitting the Parmesan cheese and lovage. Stir 2-3 tbsp of pesto into the yolk mixture before folding in the egg whites.

THYME SOUFFLÉS IN ARTICHOKES Serves 4

Miniature soufflés puffed up in their artichoke nests are perfect for an elegant lunch or brunch.

4 globe artichokes
juice of 1 lemon
40g (1½oz/3 tbsp) butter
30g (1¼oz/2½ tbsp) flour
300ml (½pt/1¼ cups) milk
4 eggs
4 tbsp freshly grated Parmesan cheese
2 tsp fresh thyme, very finely chopped
salt and pepper

Bring a large pan of water to the boil. Add 2 tbsp of salt and the lemon juice. Break the stalks from the artichokes and discard. Rub the artichokes with the cut squeezed lemon halves. Place the artichokes in the boiling water and boil until tender, about 15-20 minutes. Drain them upside down. When they are cool pull out the centre cone and choke, leaving the outer leaves to form a cup. Snip off about ½ in of the remaining outer leaves with scissors to make a straight edge. Wrap a piece of foil around the outside leaves to protect them from the oven heat.

Preheat the oven to 190°C/375°F/Gas Mark 5. Melt the butter in a small saucepan, stir in the flour and let it froth for a minute. Whisk in the milk all in one go and continue to whisk until the mixture thickens. Remove from the heat and stir in the thyme and the egg yolks, one at a time. Stir in

Lovage soufflé

Thyme soufflés in artichokes

the cheese. Whisk the egg whites with a pinch of salt until stiff and fold into the yolk mixture. Fill the artichoke cups half full and place on a baking dish. Bake for about 20 minutes, or until the soufflés have risen but are still a bit wobbly.

TERRINE OF SALMON, HERBS AND CUCUMBER
Serves 6-8

1kg (2lb) tailpiece of salmon
1.25kg (3lb) bones, heads from white fish and salmon
225ml (8floz/1 cup) dry white wine
1 small carrot, sliced
1 onion, sliced
1 bunch of parsley
2 tsp gelatine
1 good bunch of chives
1 good bunch of chervil
1 small bunch of tarragon
half cucumber, peeled and thinly sliced
salt and pepper

For the sauce
450ml (¾pt/1½ cups) mayonnaise
1 tbsp green peppercorns
Salt, pepper and lemon juice

Brush a piece of foil with oil, season the salmon, place on the foil and twist the edges together to make a baggy but tightly closed parcel. Place the parcel in a saucepan and add cold water to within 2½cm (1in) of the top. Bring the water to the boil, let it give 4 or 5 good bubblings then remove from the heat but leave the fish in the water to cool.

Remove the bones and skin from the salmon and put them in a saucepan along with the other fish bones, carrot, onion, stalks from the parsley and wine. Add just enough water to barely cover and simmer for 25 minutes. Strain then boil rapidly to reduce to 750ml (1¼pt/3 cups).

Wash and dry the herbs. Divide all the herbs in half and place half in a sieve. Pour boiling water over the herbs, drain and purée in a blender for the sauce. Chop the remaining herbs and mix with the flaked salmon. Season with salt and pepper. Place the gelatine in a small cup with 1 tbsp of cold water. Leave to sponge then place the cup in simmering water until the gelatine has dissolved. Mix the gelatine with the reduced stock. Pour a thin layer of stock in the bottom of a soufflé dish and refrigerate until it is nearly set. Place slices of cucumber over this and spoon a little stock over the cucumber. Refrigerate for a few minutes. Meanwhile mix the remaining stock into the salmon and season if necessary. Spoon the salmon over the cucumber and refrigerate until set.

Add the puréed herbs and green peppercorns to the mayonnaise and season. Place the soufflé dish in boiling water for a minute or two before turning out and serving.

JAMBON PERSILLÉ   *Serves 10-12*

1.8kg (4lb) piece of gammon
1 pig's trotter, split
450g (1lb) veal bones
1 carrot, sliced
1 stalk of celery, sliced
1 onion, quartered
8 peppercorns
bouquet garni – sprigs of parsley, bay leaf, leek and thyme tied together
1 bottle dry white wine
8 tbsp very finely chopped fresh parsley
salt and pepper

If the ham is very salty soak it overnight in cold water. Place the ham, pig's trotter and veal bones in a large saucepan and cover with cold water. Bring to the boil, and boil for 5 minutes. Drain and rinse the ham, trotter and bones under cold water. Return them to the saucepan and add the carrot, celery, onion, bouquet garni, wine and enough water to cover. Bring to the boil, skim if necessary, and simmer very gently for 2-3 hours, or until the ham is very tender.

Drain off the liquid through a muslin-lined sieve. Remove any surface fat by blotting with paper towels. Taste for seasoning. Spoon a little of the liquid on to a saucer and refrigerate to test the set. If it is too light reduce the liquid until you have a firmer set. Remove the skin from the gammon and discard it. Cut the meat into small cubes with a sharp knife and mix with the parsley. Place a layer of meat loosely in a 1.7 l (3 pt) bowl or terrine and spoon over just enough liquid to cover. Refrigerate until the liquid begins to set and then layer with ham and liquid again, continuing in this way until all the meat is used. Cover and refrigerate until firmly set. To unmould set in very hot water for a minute, run a knife around the edge before turning out on to a plate. It will keep, refrigerated, for at least 10 days.

Jambon persillé

Fish
Salmon en Croûte with Spinach and Sorrel Stuffing
Serves 8

A good-sized piece of salmon, boned and skinned is stuffed, wrapped in several sheets of buttered filo pastry and baked. The salmon stays beautifully moist and is easy to serve in attractive slices.

1kg (2lb) centre piece of salmon, boned and skinned
50g (2oz/4 tbsp) butter
small bunch of spring onions (scallions), chopped fine
1 clove garlic, chopped fine
150g (5oz/1 cup) chopped cooked fresh spinach
100g (3½oz/½ cup) chopped, cooked fresh sorrel (if unavailable use spinach)
50g (2 oz/¾ cup) soft brown breadcrumbs
4 tbsp whipping cream
lemon juice if not using sorrel
salt and freshly ground black pepper
6 sheets of filo pastry
40g (1½oz/4 tbsp) melted butter

Run your fingers against the grain of the salmon flesh to find any remaining bones. Pull them out with tweezers or a potato peeler. Season both sides of the salmon with salt and pepper.

Melt the butter and sauté the garlic and spring onions until soft but not coloured. Tip in the spinach and sorrel and stir over high heat to evaporate most of the moisture. Off heat stir in the breadcrumbs and cream, and season with salt and pepper.

Spread the mixture along the inside of one half of the salmon and then place the other half on top. Unroll the filo leaves and brush 6 slices, one at a time, with the melted butter, stacking them in a pile as you go. Place a baking sheet in the centre of the oven and preheat to 190°C/375°F/Gas Mark 5. Place the salmon in the centre of the filo and cover with each side of filo. Fold the edges under the package and brush with butter. Place on a baking sheet and set on the hot oven sheet. Bake for 25 minutes. Allow to rest for at least 5 minutes before cutting into 8 slices with a sharp serrated knife using a sawing motion. This helps keep the slices neat.

Steamed Trout Parcels with Chive Sauce
Serves 6

Other fish fillets can be used for this recipe and the stuffing can also be varied. Matchsticks of fennel softened first in a bit of oil or butter is a good alternative and mixed chopped herbs with breadcrumbs and butter another.

2 shallots, very finely chopped
1 tbsp oil
175g (6oz) mushrooms, finely chopped
squeeze of lemon juice
salt and pepper
8 large lettuce leaves
6 large pink trout fillets, skinned

For the sauce
15g (½oz/1 tbsp) butter
150g (¼pt/½ cup) white wine
150g (¼pt/½ cup) fish stock
150g (¼ pt/½ cup) double cream
3 tbsp finely snipped chives
salt and pepper

Sweat half the shallots in the oil. Add the mushrooms, lemon juice, salt and pepper. Sauté until the mushrooms give off their juices, then boil hard until all the juices have evaporated.

Blanch the lettuce by placing in a colander and pouring boiling water over it. Drain on tea towels.

Trim the fillets and remove any bones with tweezers. By running your finger against the grain of the flesh, you can feel where they are. Pat the fillets dry and season. Place a spoonful of mushrooms on the fillet and roll up. Wrap in a lettuce leaf and place seam down in a steaming basket. Steam for 20 minutes.

For the Sauce
Sweat the remaining shallot in the butter, pour in the wine and reduce by half. Add the fish stock and reduce, then add the cream and simmer until it thickens slightly. Stir in the chives and season. Serve poured over the fish parcels.

The fish parcels can be assembled ahead of time and the sauce made in advance.

GRILLED RED MULLET
WITH FENNEL SAUCE   *Serves 4*

Sauces made with puréed vegetables are both light and healthy. Fennel works very successfully and is a delicious accompaniment to grilled, steamed or baked fish. The heads and bones from the mullet can be used to make the fish stock needed for this recipe.

1 shallot, very finely chopped
15g (½oz/1 tbsp) butter

1 medium sized fennel bulb
150ml (¼ pt/⅔ cup) good fish or chicken stock
1 egg yolk
1 tbsp cream
8 red mullet fillets

Using a small heavy bottomed saucepan sweat the shallot in the butter until soft. Remove any coarse outer stalks from the fennel and save along with any green feathery tops. Cut the remaining fennel into thin slices, add to the pan, and stir for a few minutes until they are well coated in the butter. Add 5 tbsp of the stock, cover, and simmer very gently until the fennel is cooked. Turn into a blender and purée, adding as much more of the stock as necessary to make a smooth mixture. Rub through a sieve into a saucepan, add any remaining stock, and adjust the seasoning. Before serving add the egg yolk mixed with the cream and stir until hot, but not boiling. Season the fish and grill on a bed of the reserved outer stalks. Chop the feathery leaves and use as a garnish.

BAKED OCEAN PERCH WITH HERB CRUST
Serves 4

Fillets of any firm fleshed fish can be used for this dish. It is a healthy, tasty and very simple way to cook fish.

4 good sized fillets of perch, skinned
5 tbsp virgin extra olive oil
juice of half a lemon
3 tbsp of mixed fresh herbs such as chives, tarragon, basil, chervil and parsley,
   very finely chopped
salt and freshly ground black pepper
50g (2oz/½ cup) breadcrumbs

Preheat the oven to 230°C/450°F/Gas Mark 8. Place the fish in an oven dish large enough for them to fit in one layer. Marinate them in the lemon juice, 1 tbsp of the oil, 1 tbsp of the herb mixture and freshly ground black pepper for 30 minutes. Meanwhile mix the breadcrumbs, oil and remaining herbs together and season with salt and pepper. Cover the fillets with a good layer of mixture, pressing it down to make a firm crust. Bake at the top of the oven, uncovered, for about 10 minutes for thick fillets, and 8 minutes for thinner ones.

MEDALLIONS OF MONKFISH WITH TOMATO AND DILL
Serves 4

Dill and tomatoes go together beautifully and provide a tasty and healthy accompaniment for lightly sautéed fish steaks.

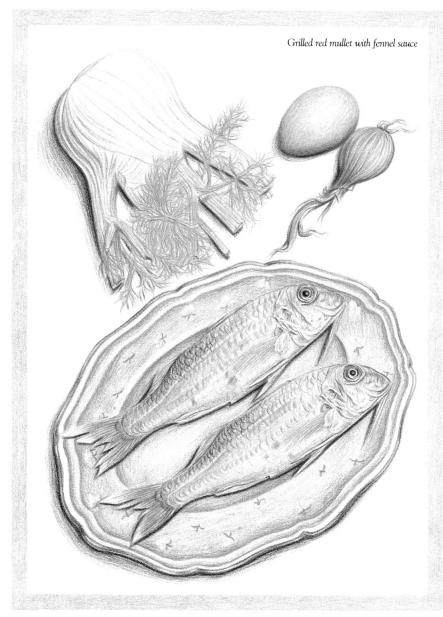

Grilled red mullet with fennel sauce

Baked ocean perch with herb crust

625g (1¼ lb) thick monkfish fillet
25g (1oz/2 tbsp) butter
8 tomatoes peeled, seeded and chopped
4 tbsp finely chopped fresh dill weed
1 tbsp olive oil
pinch of sugar
2 tbsp dry white wine
salt and pepper

Remove the skin from the monkfish fillets and cut into equal size medallions. Mix the tomatoes, dill, oil and sugar together and season with salt and pepper. Heat the butter in a frying pan until it is bubbling hot and sauté the fish for a few minutes each side, until just cooked. Remove to a heated dish. Deglaze the pan with the wine then stir in the tomatoes to just heat through. Serve the medallions with the sauce spooned over the top.

SOLE FILLETS WITH SORREL SAUCE   *Serves 4*

2 handfuls of sorrel
125ml (4 fl oz/½ cup) muscadet
125ml (4 fl oz/½ cup) Nouilly Prat Vermouth
125ml (4 fl oz/½ cup) fish stock
150ml (¼ pt/⅔ cup) double cream
squeeze of lemon juice
salt and pepper
4 sole fillets, skinned
a few leaves of lemon balm or parsley

Wash the sorrel and pull off the stalks and central ribs. Roll up like cigars and cut into very thin slices. Boil the muscadet, Nouilly and fish stock together to evaporate the alcohol and reduce by half. Stir in the cream and simmer for a few minutes until it thickens slightly. Season with salt and pepper. This can be prepared ahead of time if you float a piece of cling-film over the sauce to prevent a skin forming. Season the fillets and lightly cook in a non-stick pan or sauté in an ordinary pan with a bit of butter. Meanwhile reheat the sauce, add the shredded sorrel and season with lemon juice, salt and pepper. Serve the fish on a pool of sauce garnished with a fine sprinkling of lemon balm or parsley.

PAPILLOTES OF SALMON
WITH CHERVIL   *Serves 6*

Fish steaks baked in papillotes keep beautifully moist and imbibe the herb flavours they are sealed with.

50g (2 oz/4 tbsp) butter, softened
2 tbsp finely chopped fresh chervil
salt and pepper
oil
6 thick salmon steaks

Mash the butter and chervil together and season well with salt and pepper. Wrap in cling-film and refrigerate until firm.

Cut 6 heart-shapes from greaseproof paper large enough to contain a steak when folded in half. Oil one half of the paper and place a well seasoned steak on it. Divide the butter into 6 pats and place on top of the fish. Seal the parcels by crimping the edges – it should be a tightly sealed but roomy parcel. (Foil can also be used.) Preheat the oven to 200°C/400°F/Gas Mark 6. Bake the parcels for 10-12 minutes. Do not overcook or the steaks will toughen.

VEGETABLES

PARSLEY PURÉE   Serves 6
A perfect accompaniment for game, especially venison.

350ml (12oz) parsley leaves
110ml (4floz/½ cup) double cream
15g (½oz/1 tbsp) butter
salt and pepper

Wash and drain the parsley. Remove the stalks before weighing. Simmer in 300ml (½pt/1¼ cups) of boiling salted water for 3 minutes. Drain then purée in a blender with the cream. Reheat with the butter and seasoning.

BAKED GRATED PARSNIPS
WITH PARSLEY   Serves 6
As delicious as this is, I don't think I would contemplate it without a processor to grate the parsnips. If you haven't one you could slice the parsnips horizontally and layer with tomatoes, butter and parsley and bake in the same way.

1 ¼kg (2½lb) parsnips
bunch of parsley
40g (1½oz) butter
salt and pepper

Peel then grate the parsnips in a processor. Butter a baking dish and layer with parsnips and a fine sprinkling of parsley dotted with butter and seasoned. Repeat these layers ending with the parsnips. Bake in a moderate oven for 45 minutes. Cover the top when it threatens to burn, but allow it to form a crunchy brown top.

COURGETTES IN TARRAGON CREAM

Cut small firm courgettes in quarters lengthwise, steam or blanch them until just cooked. Before serving heat them in a few tablespoons of cream and some chopped fresh tarragon.

FRIED PARSLEY

This is one of the nicest accompaniments for fish and worth the trouble of deep frying.

2-3 sprays of parsley per person
oil for deep-frying
salt

Remove any tough parsley stalks. Wash well in cold water and spin dry, then pat dry with paper towels. Heat the oil to 185°C/360°F. Add the parsley, a handful at a time, and cook for about 45 seconds. Keep the parsley submerged with a slotted spoon if necessary. Drain on paper towels, sprinkle with salt and serve hot.

BAKED BASIL POTATOES   *Serves 8*

A perfect way of making extra special potatoes ahead of time. They only need to be reheated before serving.

4 good-sized baking potatoes
50g (2oz/4 tbsp) butter
150ml (¼ pt/⅔ cup) double cream
2 small eggs, separated
20 basil leaves
50g (2oz/6 tbsp) freshly grated Parmesan cheese
good squeeze of lemon juice
salt and freshly ground black pepper

Bake the potatoes in the usual way. When they are cool enough to handle cut them in half, scoop out the insides and sieve through a vegetable mill into a bowl. Stir in the butter, cream and egg yolks. Shred the basil leaves by hand and add to the potatoes along with the cheese. Whisk the egg whites with a pinch of salt and fold into the potatoes then season to taste with salt and lots of pepper. Pile the mixture back into the skins and set in a low oven dish. Bake them in a hot oven for around 15 minutes, or until heated through. They can be made 2 days ahead if kept refrigerated.

SALSIFY WITH CHIVES
Serves 4

16 salsify stalks
1 tbsp butter
1 tbsp chives
salt and freshly ground pepper

Peel the roots under running water and cut into cigarette-size pieces. Place in a heavy-bottomed saucepan with the butter and some salt and pepper. Simmer, covered, over the lowest possible heat. Shake the pan occasionally, but the salsify will give off its own moisture and cook beautifully if the heat is gentle enough. Stir in the chives and serve.

BAKED TOMATOES WITH BASIL AND CREAM
Serves 6

12 large tomatoes, peeled
salt and pepper
sugar
15-20 basil leaves, torn into small pieces
300ml (½ pt) double cream
60g (2½oz/½ cup) breadcrumbs
25g (1oz/2 tbsp) butter

Slice the tomatoes and place a layer in a gratin dish. Season with salt, pepper and sugar. Cover with some cream and basil leaves. Continue until the tomatoes and cream are used up. Sprinkle over the breadcrumbs and dot with butter. Bake in a moderate oven for about 35 minutes.

BRUSSEL SPROUTS WITH MARJORAM

Cook sprouts in the usual way then toss them in hot butter and chopped marjoram.

HOT DILL POTATOES VINAIGRETTE

This is my favourite potato dish and with the emphasis today on olive oil for health I can indulge myself with a clear conscience.

Boil or steam new scrubbed (not peeled) potatoes in the usual way until they are well cooked and will break quite easily with a fork. While they are still piping hot mix with a vinaigrette to which you have added lots of chopped dill weed. Season with salt and pepper. As you stir in the vinaigrette the potatoes should break up a little so the vinaigrette is soaked up by the potatoes.

Salads

Lentil and Coriander Salad   *Serves 8-10*

450g (1lb) tiny brown or green lentils
1 onion stuck with 2 cloves
1 carrot, quartered
1 stalk of celery, quartered
bouquet garni
4 tbsp mango or other fruit chutney
good bunch of fresh coriander leaves, very finely chopped

For the vinaigrette
110ml (4fl oz) olive oil or half sunflower and half olive oil
4-5 tbsp balsamic or tarragon vinegar
salt and freshly ground black pepper

Pick over the lentils for any grit, then rinse in a few changes of water. Place in a large saucepan with 1 ⅔ l (3 pt) of water, the onion, carrot, celery and bouquet garni. Bring to the boil and skim if necessary. Lower the heat, cover, and simmer very gently for about 25 minutes or until the lentils are tender but still hold their shape. It is important not to overcook them. Drain, discard the vegetables and bouquet garni. Pour into the bowl you intend to serve them in.

Mix the vinaigrette ingredients together, season very well, and pour over the lentils. Fold in the chutney and the coriander and adjust the seasoning. If you are preparing this ahead of time save half the coriander in an air-tight container and add just before serving.

Chervil, Chicory and Grape Salad *Serves 6*

4 firm heads of chicory
150g (5oz) Italia grapes, peeled and pipped
1 tsp Dijon mustard
5 tbsp double cream
1 tbsp lemon juice
salt and freshly ground black pepper
1-2 tbsp finely chopped fresh chervil

Slice the chicory and mix with the grapes. Mix the other ingredients together and toss with the salad.

Nasturtium Salad

A handful of bright nasturtium flowers adds a cheerful note and slight peppery taste when added to salads. The flowers can also provide an enchanting salad on their own with the addition of a few nasturtium buds and chopped leaves. It goes particularly well with a dressing made with some fresh chervil, salt, lemon juice and olive oil.

FLOWER SALADS

Nasturtium flowers are not the only edible flowers. Sage, bergamot, anchusa, rosemary, lavender, borage and mimosa are just some of the flowers that can be added to salads. Petals from both roses and marigolds will also add flavour and elegance to the salad bowl.

HERBS IN SALADS

Green salads can be greatly enhanced by the inclusion of a fresh herb or two. They can transform an ordinary salad into one with fragrance and character. You only want a suspicion of the flavour to come through the salad – it should not dominate it – so very few leaves may do the trick, depending on the strength of the herb. Use young tender leaves if possible and experiment with what is available. Lovage, angelica, bergamot, hyssop, dill, sweet cecily, lemon balm, chervil, tarragon and basil are just some of the possibilities. Purslane and rocket can be used in larger amounts. Use a good selection of the salad greens now available such as oakleafed lettuce, chicory, tom thumb, escarole and radici. Lamb's lettuce, or corn salad as it is also known by, is particularly delicious and very easy to grow. It will continue through much of the winter from sowings made in August or early September.

DANDELION SALAD WITH BACON
Salade de Pissenlit au Lard   *Serves 6*

Choose only very young dandelion leaves and don't be tempted to taste them until after they are dressed. The warm dressing tenderizes the leaves and takes the edge off their bitterness.

2-5mm (¼in) slices of streaky bacon, cut crosswise into 5 mm slices
250g (8oz) young dandelion leaves, washed and dried
2 tbsp olive oil
2 tbsp mild tarragon wine vinegar
salt and freshly ground black pepper
2 dandelion flowers

Blanch the bacon by throwing it into boiling water and boiling for 1 minute. Refresh under cold water and drain. Heat the oil in a frying pan and sauté the bacon until it is golden. Add the vinegar to the pan and the moment it boils stir in the dandelion leaves. When they start to wilt turn them into a warmed ceramic salad bowl. Season with salt and pepper and toss. Scatter the petals from the flowers over the salad and serve immediately.

PASTA AND GRAINS

LINGUINE WITH MINT AND PRAWNS   *Serves 4-5*

It sounds unlikely but this is an Italian dish and its combination of curry, mint and prawns is quite delicious.

350g (12oz) linguine or spaghettini
75g (3oz/6 tbsp) butter
350g (12oz) fresh or frozen peeled prawns, thawed if frozen
1 tbsp curry powder
4 tbsp white wine
300ml (½ pt/1¼ cups) fish or chicken stock
2 egg yolks and 1 whole egg
100g (4oz) freshly grated Parmesan cheese
4 tbsp finely chopped fresh mint leaves
salt and freshly ground black pepper

Bring a large quantity of water to the boil, add 4 tbsp of salt and throw in the pasta. Cover the pot until the water returns to the boil then continue to cook uncovered.

Meanwhile heat half the butter in a large frying pan and stir in the curry powder. Stir in the prawns and cook just long enough to heat through. Add the wine and boil over a fierce heat to reduce, then add the stock. Mix the eggs and cheese with half the mint in a small bowl.

When the pasta is cooked *al dente* drain lightly and pour into the frying pan. Cut the remaining butter into pieces and add together with the egg mixture. Stir over a low heat until the sauce thickens and coats the pasta. Season to taste, toss with the rest of the mint and serve.

TAGLIATELLE WITH SCALLOPS AND PARSLEY SAUCE   *Serves 4*

This sauce deserves the best fresh pasta available – homemade if possible.

350g (12oz) fresh tagliatelle
1 shallot, very finely chopped
50g (2oz/4 tbsp) butter
1 tbsp olive oil
60g (2½oz/½ cup) fresh parsley leaves, very finely chopped

175ml (6fl oz/¾ cup) dry white wine
350g (12oz) sea scallops, fresh or defrosted if frozen
350ml (12fl oz/1½ cups) single cream
75g (3oz) freshly grated Parmesan cheese
grated nutmeg
salt and freshly ground black pepper

The sauce is so quick to make that the water for cooking the pasta can be brought to the boil as you make the sauce. Heat the butter and oil in a frying pan over low heat. Add the shallot and cook, stirring, until it softens then stir in half the parsley. Add the wine and reduce by half. Slice each scallop horizontally into three discs. Add the slices along with the corals to the pan and stir over moderately high heat for 1 minute. Remove the scallops with a slotted spoon, season with salt and pepper and set aside. Add the cream to the pan and simmer for about 2 minutes. Remove from the heat and stir in the rest of the parsley, the cheese, a few gratings of nutmeg, salt and pepper. Keep the sauce warm while you cook the pasta. Drain the pasta in a colander placed over the bowl you plan to serve it in. This will warm it nicely. Tip the hot water out of the bowl and pour in the drained pasta. Add the sauce and scallops. Toss well and serve immediately.

RISOTTO WITH HERBS   *Serves 4*

You have to be prepared to stir, on and off, for about 25 minutes to achieve a true creamy Italian risotto. Make the salad, grate the cheese, chop the herbs but keep a close eye on the rice – topping it up with broth and stirring as needed. It is well worth the effort.

2 shallots very finely chopped
50g (2oz/4 tbsp) butter
350g (12oz/1¾ cups) Arborio rice
1½ l (3 pt) chicken stock
8-10 tbsp finely chopped mixed fresh herbs such as basil, chives, chervil, tarragon,
    parsley, mint, sage (use a small amount), marjoram and thyme
50g (2oz/¾ cup) freshly grated Parmesan cheese
salt and freshly ground black pepper

Bring the stock to a simmer. Using a heavy-bottomed saucepan sauté the shallot in half the butter until soft, add the rice and stir over medium heat for 1 or 2 minutes to coat the rice with fat. Add one cup of simmering broth, stirring until the rice has absorbed the liquid and is threatening to stick. Add half a cup of stock and stir on and off until it is absorbed. Continue adding the stock by the half cupful, stirring and keeping a watchful eye so it doesn't stick. Keep the heat about medium. You may have to adjust the amount of liquid, adding more stock or water if the rice needs it or holding back on some if it is too much. The risotto should have a creamy consistency yet not be swimming in liquid, and the rice tender but firm when it is done. Stir in the rest of the butter, a few tablespoons of cheese and the herbs. Season with pepper and salt if necessary. Cover the pan and leave the risotto for 2 minutes to let the herbs flavour the rice, then serve immediately in warm bowls with the remaining cheese passed separately.

BULGHUR WITH HERBS   *Serves 4-6*

100g (4oz) each of finely chopped carrot, onion, and celery
50g (2oz/4 tbsp) butter
2 tbsp oil
small bunch of fresh parsley, finely chopped
1 tbsp chopped fresh marjoram
1 tsp chopped fresh thyme
grated rind of one lemon
juice of ½ lemon
450g (1lb) coarse bulghur
1l (1¾pt) water
50g (2oz) pine nuts
salt and freshly ground black pepper
3 tbsp chopped fresh coriander leaves

Using a large frying pan, sauté the vegetables in half the butter until soft. Add the rest of the butter and the oil and stir in the bulghur until well coated in the fat. Add half the parsley, all the marjoram and thyme and the lemon rind and juice. Pour in the water, season, and bring to the boil. Simmer, covered, very gently for about 25 minutes. The water should be absorbed and the grains separated. Turn into an oven dish, sprinkle with pine nuts and bake in a moderate oven for about 15 minutes. Stir in the coriander and remaining parsley and serve.

Bulghur with herbs

MEAT, POULTRY AND GAME

BRAISED RABBIT WITH SAGE
AND TOMATO

Serves 4

An infusion made with sage is used for braising the rabbit. It flavours the
rabbit and with the tomatoes provides a delicious sauce.

1kg (2lb) rabbit pieces
300ml (½ pt/1¼ cups) water
30 fresh sage leaves
25g (1oz/2 tbsp) butter
1 tbsp olive oil
3 tbsp dry white wine
salt and freshly ground black pepper
3 tomatoes, skinned, seeded and chopped
1 tsp arrowroot
2 tbsp cream

Bring the water to the boil. Add all but 4 of the sage leaves, cover and leave
off the heat to infuse for 15 minutes. Finely chop the remaining sage leaves
and set aside.

Meanwhile brown the rabbit pieces in the butter and oil. Remove the browned pieces and deglaze the pan with the wine. Return the rabbit to the pan, pour over the strained infusion and season well with salt and pepper. Simmer over very low heat, covered, for about 20 minutes or until the rabbit is just tender. Remove the rabbit to a heated serving dish and keep warm in a low oven. Add the tomatoes to the liquid left in the pan and cook briskly for a minute or two. Slake the arrowroot in a bit of cold water and add to the pan along with the cream and chopped sage. Taste for seasoning then pour over the rabbit and serve.

CHICKEN BREASTS WITH RED WINE AND TARRAGON
Serves 4

50g (2oz/4 tbsp) unsalted butter
4 chicken breasts, boned and skinned
2 tbsp chopped fresh tarragon plus 4 sprigs
300ml (½ pt) Brouilly or good Beaujolais
salt and pepper

Pat the breasts dry and season. Heat half the butter in a non-stick frying pan. Sauté the breasts over medium heat for about 7 minutes each side. Remove the breasts from the pan and keep warm. Add the tarragon and wine to the pan and quickly reduce by half. Remove the pan from the heat, add the remaining butter cut into tiny pieces and swirl the pan to blend the butter into the sauce. This should thicken the sauce and prevent the butter from going oily. Adjust for seasoning. Place the breasts on four warmed plates and coat with the sauce. Garnish with the tarragon sprigs.

CHICKEN BREASTS STUFFED WITH HERB CHEESE
Serves 6

This is somewhat like chicken Kiev with the usual butter filling replaced by a lighter herby curd cheese.

8 tbsp curd cheese
1 tbsp fresh tarragon, chopped
1 tbsp fresh chives, very finely chopped
1 tsp parsley, finely chopped
salt and freshly ground black pepper
6 boned and skinned chicken breasts
1 egg, lightly beaten
75g (3oz/½ cup) breadcrumbs
50g (2oz/4 tbsp) clarified butter
5 tbsp sunflower or groundnut oil

Mix the herbs with the cheese and season with salt and pepper. Detach the small, feather-shaped fillet from the breasts. Flatten the breasts and fillets by beating lightly with a wet rolling pin. Season the breasts with salt and pepper. Place a spoonful of the cheese on the breast, lay the fillet over the top and tuck in all the ends to make a parcel. Season the breadcrumbs with salt and pepper. Roll the breasts in the beaten egg then in the crumbs. Refrigerate the breasts if you are not cooking them immediately.

Using a large, heavy-bottomed frying pan heat the butter and oil until it is bubbling. Add the breasts and cook over moderate heat, first on one side and then the other until done, about 6 or 7 minutes each side. They should be firm but still springy to the touch.

Note: Herb butters can also be used as stuffings.

PIGEON BREASTS WITH THYME SAUCE   Serves 4

Pigeons are relatively inexpensive. The breasts are the meatiest part so it is not too extravagant to use the rest of the bird for a delicious sauce.

4 pigeons
2 fl oz/6 tbsp red wine
1 onion, sliced
½ stalk of celery, chopped
1 carrot, chopped
2 tbsp olive oil
bay leaf
a few parsley stalks
3 sprigs of thyme, fresh or dried
15g (½oz/1 tbsp) butter
½ tsp fresh thyme leaves, chopped finely (or ¼ tsp dried)
2 tbsp cream
1 tbsp arrowroot
salt and freshly ground black papper

Remove the breast from the pigeons and place in the red wine to marinate. Chop three of the carcasses into pieces and brown in half the oil in a large heavy frying pan. Remove the pieces to a saucepan. Brown the vegetables in the frying pan and add them to the saucepan along with the bayleaf, parsley, and sprigs of thyme. Cover with cold water, bring to the boil, skim if necessary and simmer gently, covered, for 1½ hours. Strain and reduce the stock to about 300ml (½ pt) then season to taste.

Remove the breasts from the marinade and reserve the marinade. Pat the breasts dry, season, and sauté in the butter and tablespoon of oil. They will only need about 4 minutes each side. Remove them from the pan and keep warm in a low oven. Pour off any fat from the pan and deglaze with a little

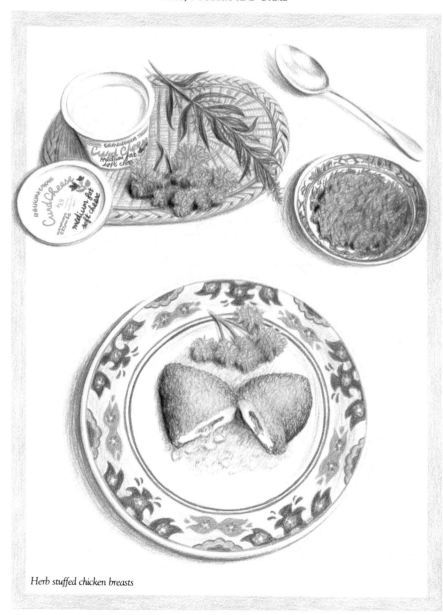

Herb stuffed chicken breasts

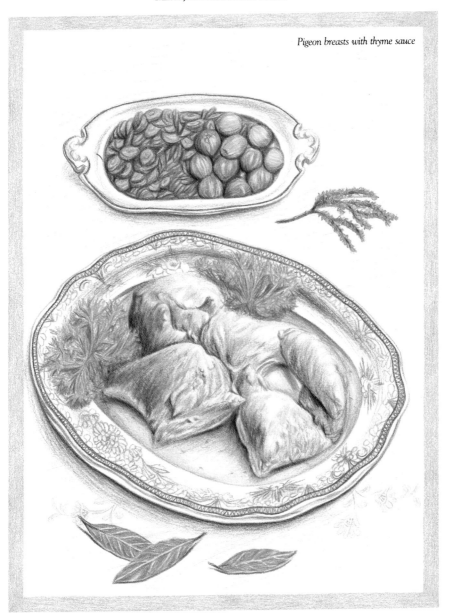

Pigeon breasts with thyme sauce

of the red wine. Add this to the stock along with the fresh thyme. Slake the arrowroot in a little cold water and add to the stock. Simmer for a few minutes to thicken then stir in the cream and taste for seasoning. Serve the breasts on a pool of sauce. Carrots and glazed shallots go well with pigeon.

MINT LAMB PARCELS   Serves 6

This easy method of baking lamb in a parcel seals in all the flavours of both mint and meat.

6 loin lamb chops, 3.8cm (1½ in) thick, boned and fat removed
3 tbsp fresh mint, very finely chopped
50g (2oz/4 tbsp) butter
½ cucumber, peeled and sliced
6 small sprigs of mint
salt and freshly ground black pepper

Mash the chopped mint with the butter. Cut out 6 heart-shapes from foil large enough to contain a chop when the heart shape is folded in half. Season the lamb with salt and pepper, place on the foil with a pat of mint butter, some cucumber slices and a sprig of mint. Seal the packages tightly but leave a bit of room inside. Preheat the oven to 180°C/350°F/Gas Mark 4. Place the parcels on a baking sheet and bake for 20 minutes.

GRILLED MARINATED CHICKEN   Serves 6

The yoghurt and herb marinade tenderizes as well as flavours the chicken breasts and provides a delicious sauce to accompany the grilled meat.

50g (2oz/⅔ cup) dessicated coconut
300ml (½ pt) yoghurt
2 large handfuls of coriander leaves
1 tbsp fresh chopped mint
1 small green chili, seeded and chopped
1 tsp sugar
squeeze of lemon juice
6 chicken breasts, boned and skinned
2 tbsp cream
salt

Place the first seven ingredients in a blender and purée until you have a thick paste. Place the chicken in a shallow dish and cover with the sauce. Leave to marinate for between 1-2 hours. Remove the chicken from the marinade and pat dry. Place under a hot grill until just cooked through. Meanwhile bring the marinade to a boil, stir in the cream and season with salt and more lemon juice if needed. Serve with the grilled chicken breasts.

STEAK WITH SHALLOT AND PARSLEY SAUCE

Serves 4

8 shallots
25g (1oz/2 tbsp) butter
1 tbsp wine vinegar
4 tenderloin or other steaks suitable for pan frying
1 tbsp oil
150ml (¼ pt) stock
½ cup chopped fresh parsley leaves
1 tbsp cream
salt and pepper

Peel the shallots then place in a small heavy-bottomed saucepan with half the butter and the vinegar. Cover and simmer very gently (use a simmering disc if necessary) until tender. Heat the remaining butter and oil until very hot in a non-stick or other heavy frying pan. Dry the steaks with paper towels and season. Cook the steaks quickly on both sides. Remove the steaks and keep warm while you make the sauce. Pour away any excess fat from the pan, add the stock and parsley and boil together for a few seconds. Tip into a blender with the shallots and purée. Adjust seasoning and add the cream. Serve in a sauceboat to accompany the steaks.

VEAL ESCALOPES STUFFED WITH HERBS *Serves 6*

A pocket is slit in veal escalopes and stuffed with herbs and ricotta. It keeps the veal moist and gives the taste a lift.

6 veal escalopes about 10 mm (⅜ in) thick
110g (4oz) fresh ricotta cheese
25g (1oz) mortadella salami, very finely chopped
16 basil leaves, finely chopped
1 tbsp finely chopped fresh parsley
salt and pepper
knob of butter
1 tbsp oil
1 lemon or lime cut into 6 wedges

Using a very sharp knife cut the escalope horizontally, to make a pocket, leaving an edge intact on three sides. Be careful not to come through the meat at any point. Mix the ricotta, mortadella and herbs together and season. Smear a layer of stuffing inside the pocket and skewer together with a toothpick. Season the meat on both sides. Heat a little oil and butter in a frying pan and when it is bubbling hot sauté the meat for 2-3 minutes on each side. Serve with a wedge of lemon.

DUCK BREASTS WITH
ROSEMARY SAUCE
Serves 6

Rosemary is delicious with duck and also goes well with lamb. The sauce below can be used with noisettes or other cuts of lamb.

6 duck breasts
sprig of rosemary
1 tbsp very finely chopped fresh rosemary
15g (½oz/1 tbsp) butter
1 shallot, very finely chopped
½ carrot, very finely chopped
½ stalk of celery, very finely chopped
small glass of white wine
300ml (½ pt/1¼ cups) duck or chicken stock
salt and pepper
1 tbsp arrowroot
1 tbsp port

Score the duck skin and rub with salt and pepper; place in an oiled tin with a sprig of rosemary on top. Roast in an oven preheated to 215°C/425°F/Gas Mark 7 for 15 minutes.

While the duck is roasting sauté the vegetables in the butter, stirring, until softened. When the breasts are done remove them to a serving dish and keep warm. Pour off any fat from the roasting tin and deglaze with the wine. Add to the vegetables and simmer until slightly reduced. Add the stock and chopped rosemary, and reduce slightly. Mix the arrowroot with the port, add to the sauce, and simmer for a minute or two. Taste for seasoning. Pour some sauce on to hot plates and set the breasts on top.

BERGAMOT PORK FILLETS
Serves 6

2 large pork fillets
75g (3oz/6 tbsp) butter
2 shallots, very finely chopped
40g (1½oz/2½tbsp) flour
300ml (½pt/1¼ cup) chicken stock
small handful of seeded raisins
4 tbsp dry white wine
3½ tbsp chopped bergamot leaves
salt and freshly ground black pepper
1 tbsp cream

Sweat the shallots in half the butter until soft. Stir in the flour and cook for a minute. Whisk in the stock and raisins, simmer until it thickens, then

Duck breasts with rosemary sauce

add the wine and 3 tbsp of the bergamot. Simmer for several minutes then season with salt and pepper.

Meanwhile preheat the oven to 200°C/400°F/Gas Mark 6. Pat the fillets dry, season and smear with the remaining butter. Roast the fillets in a greased shallow tin for 25 minutes. Allow them to rest for 5 minutes before slicing. Deglaze the pan with a little sauce, reheat the sauce adding the deglazed sauce and stir in the cream. Serve the fillets with the sauce garnished with the remaining chopped bergamot.

CALVES LIVER WITH SAGE AND AVOCADO
Serves 4

This is such an easy and quick dish to prepare that it is ideal for occasions when you are too busy to do any preparation in advance.

625g (1¼lb) calves liver, thinly sliced
25g (1oz/2 tbsp) butter
2 tbsp olive oil
well seasoned flour
12 fresh young sage leaves, roughly chopped
1 ripe avocado pear
salt and freshly ground black pepper
4 tbsp Marsala or medium dry sherry

Dry the slices of liver with paper towelling and remove any fibrous pieces. Roll them in the flour shaking off any excess. Cook the liver in two batches, or better still divide the butter and oil between two frying pans. Place over medium heat and when the fat is sizzling add the liver slices. Sprinkle over the sage and sauté for about 2 minutes, just long enough to seal the surface. Turn the slices, add the avocado and season with salt and pepper. Sauté for only a minute or two before removing the liver and avocado slices to four warmed serving plates. Pour the alcohol into the pans and scrape up any bits clinging to the pan before pouring over the liver. Serve immediately.

LEG OF LAMB WITH ROSEMARY AND MUSTARD CRUST
Serves 8

If possible coat the lamb several hours before roasting and leave at room temperature.

2¼ kg (5lb) leg of lamb
1 shallot, finely chopped
1 clove garlic, finely chopped
2 tbsp olive oil

125ml (4 fl oz) Dijon mustard
2 tbsp soya sauce
1 tsp grated fresh ginger
1 tbsp very finely chopped fresh rosemary or half quantity dried
1 tbsp finely chopped fresh parsley
salt

Gently sweat the shallot and garlic in the oil, stirring, until they have softened, then stir into the other ingredients. Rub the lamb with salt then paint with the mustard mixture. Set on a rack in a roasting pan and roast in a preheated oven set at 180°C/350°F/Gas Mark 4, for 1½ hours for a medium-done roast. Let it rest for at least 5 minutes before carving.

ROAST LOIN OF PORK WITH FRESH CORIANDER AND LEMON STUFFING   *Serves 6*

Sue Oury, a friend and inspired cook, is responsible for this delicious recipe.

2kg (4½lb) boned loin of pork

Stuffing
125g (4oz) fresh white breadcrumbs
grated rind of one lemon
juice of half a lemon
2 tbsp of finely chopped fresh coriander
1 clove garlic, crushed
25g (1oz/2 tbsp) melted butter
1 beaten egg
salt and freshly ground black pepper
2 tbsp oil
fresh coriander leaves and lemon slices to garnish

Mix together the breadcrumbs, grated lemon rind, fresh coriander and garlic. Stir in the lemon juice and melted butter then bind togther with the beaten egg and season well with salt and pepper.

Open out the meat on a board and score the rind with a sharp knife in a criss-cross pattern. Turn the meat over and cover with the stuffing. Roll up the meat to reform the loin and tie in several places to keep the stuffing in place.

Preheat the oven to 220°C/425°F/Gas Mark 7. Rub the rind with salt and place in a roasting tin with 2 tbsp of oil. Cook for 15 minutes then reduce the heat to 190°C/375°F/Gas Mark 5 and cook a further 1½ hours. Remove the meat from the oven and leave it for 10 minutes to rest. Carve the meat in neat slices and arrange overlapping on a warm serving plate. Garnish with fresh coriander leaves and lemon slices.

A gravy can be made by pouring off the fat from the roasting tin and deglazing with a little white wine and stock.

TONGUE WITH CREAM OF PARSLEY SAUCE

Serves 6-8

1²/₃ kg (4lb) salt ox tongue
1 carrot, chopped
1 onion, chopped
1 celery stalk, chopped
2 bay leaves
parsley stalks
25g (1oz/2 tbsp) butter
1 shallot, chopped very fine
125ml (4 fl oz) dry white wine
150ml (5 fl oz) tongue stock
50g (2oz) parsley without stalks
175ml (6 fl oz) double cream
salt and freshly ground black pepper
bunch of watercress

Soak the tongue overnight in cold water to cover. The next day drain the tongue, place in a large saucepan with the carrot, onion, celery, bay leaves and parsley stalks. Cover with fresh cold water, bring to the boil, cover, and simmer gently for 4 hours, or until the tongue is very tender. Allow the tongue to cool slightly in the stock before lifting it out and peeling it. Strain the stock and pour back into the washed saucepan. Place the tongue back in the stock to keep warm while you make the sauce. Sauté the shallot in the butter, over gentle heat, until it is soft. Pour in the wine and reduce by half. Add 150ml (5 fl oz) of the tongue stock to the wine. When it comes to the boil throw in the parsley. Boil for a minute or two to tenderize the parsley then pour the contents of the pan into a blender and purée. Return the purée to the pan and stir in enough cream to make a thin sauce. Season with pepper and salt if it needs it. Drain the tongue and slice it. Place the slices on a heated platter garnished with branches of watercress. Serve with the hot parsley sauce.

SAUCES

BASIL SAUCE
PESTO ALLA GENOVESE

Makes enough for
675g (1½lb) of pasta

Pesto is traditionally made in a mortar and pestle (from which it gets its name), but the blender method is so easy and delicious that I fully recommend it. Pesto freezes very successfully if you leave out the garlic, butter and cheese and add it later when thawed. It is wonderful to have on hand to serve with pasta or to use with fish, soups or stews. A little goes a long way so use sparingly. This amount will be enough for 675g (1½lbs) of pasta.

50g (2 oz/2 cups) fresh basil leaves, without any coarse stalks
110ml (4 fl oz/½ cup) olive oil
50g (2 oz/5 tbsp) pine nuts
2 cloves garlic, peeled
½ tsp salt
50g (2oz/4 tbsp) butter
100g (4oz/¾ cup) freshly grated Parmesan cheese

Purée the basil, oil, nuts, garlic and salt in a blender or food processor. Transfer to a bowl and mix in the butter and cheese. Add 7-8 tbsp of the water used for cooking the pasta to the sauce before mixing with the pasta.

CORIANDER SAUCE AND STUFFING

This is great with just about everything; potatoes, pasta, fish and meat. Use it to stuff a boned leg of lamb and serve some in a bowl as an accompaniment.

1 clove garlic, finely chopped
250g (8oz) mushrooms
virgin extra olive oil
squeeze of lemon juice
75g (3oz/1 cup) fresh coriander leaves, chopped
3 tbsp pine nuts
½ cup breadcrumbs
1 egg
salt and pepper

Sweat the garlic in a few tablespoons of the oil without allowing it to colour. Stir in the sliced mushrooms, season with salt and pepper and lemon juice and simmer until the mushrooms are tender. Scrape them into a blender with the chopped coriander leaves and pine nuts. Blend with just enough oil to make a purée. Add the breadcrumbs and egg and whizz again. Season generously with salt and pepper, adjusting the consistency with more oil if necessary. Scrape into a bowl and use as a stuffing and relish.

GREEN SAUCE
Serves 6

A sauce from Jane Grigson's *Fish Cookery* which she in turn found in *Gastronomie Normande*, by Simone Morand (Flammarion, 1970). Try it with mackerel or cod.

3 shallots, finely chopped
2 cloves garlic, finely chopped
75g (3oz/6 tbsp) butter
1 tbsp Dijon mustard
dash of mild wine vinegar
125ml (4 floz/½ cup) double cream
2 tbsp of finely chopped fresh parsley, plus more if necessary
1 tbsp finely chopped fresh tarragon, plus more if necessary
salt and pepper

Gently simmer the shallots, garlic and 2 tbsp of parsley in the butter until the shallots soften. Stir in the mustard and vinegar then add the cream and tablespoon of tarragon. Continue to cook until the sauce thickens. Season it well and adjust the flavouring by adding more herbs, vinegar or mustard. The sauce should be strongly flavoured and have a nice green colour.

TOMATO SAUCE WITH MARJORAM
Makes 600ml (1 pt)

Tomato sauce is delicious with pasta, and can also serve as a sauce for fish. A variety of fresh herbs can be used in place of the marjoram.

5 tbsp extra virgin olive oil
1 medium sized onion, chopped
1 carrot, sliced
1 stick of celery, chopped
2 x 400g (14oz) can of peeled, chopped tomatoes
1 tsp sugar
1 tbsp fresh chopped sweet marjoram
salt and freshly ground black pepper

Sauté the vegetables in 2 tbsp of the oil until they are slightly soft. Add the tomatoes and sugar and simmer covered for 1 hour. Purée through a blender or press through a sieve. Return the sauce to the pan, add the remaining oil and marjoram and taste for seasoning.

TOMATO SAUCE WITH ROSEMARY AND BACON
Makes 600ml (1 pt)

Add 250g (8oz) of unsmoked back bacon or pancetta, cut into lardoons, to the list of ingredients for Tomato Sauce with Marjoram and substitute 2 tsp of very finely chopped fresh rosemary for the marjoram. Follow the directions for making the sauce up to sieving it. Heat the remaining 3 tbsp of olive oil in a frying pan, add the bacon and sauté until brown. Stir in the rosemary and add the sieved sauce. Season, and serve hot with pasta.

BAKES

ITALIAN FLAT BREAD WITH SAGE

This bread is so good eaten on its own that there is no need for butter. A great plus if you are trying to cut back on dairy products.

25g (1oz) fresh yeast, or half quantity dried yeast
2 tsp salt
450g (1lb) strong white unbleached flour
5 tbsp extra virgin olive oil
12 fresh sage leaves, chopped

Dissolve the yeast in a scant 300 ml (½ pt/1¼ cups) of lukewarm water. Mix the salt with the flour, make a well in the centre and add the yeasty water and 4 tbsp of the olive oil. Knead until the dough is smooth and elastic. This can also be done in a food processor. Place the dough in a lightly oiled bowl, cover with a plastic bag and leave to rise in a warm place until more than doubled in size.

Knock the dough down and knead again, this time adding the sage or other herb. Place a heavy metal baking sheet in the oven and preheat to 200°C/400°F/Gas Mark 6. Shape the dough into a flatish circle about 30cm (12in) in diameter. When the oven has reached the correct temperature dimple the surface of the dough with your finger and dribble the remaining oil over it. Either slide a floured board under the bread and then quickly slide it off on to the hot baking sheet, or pick it up with your hands and toss it on to the sheet. It doesn't matter if the shape becomes irregular. Bake for about 35 minutes or until a deep golden colour. Cool on a rack, then wrap and keep in a bread tin. Reheat for 10 minutes in a hot oven before serving or serve as it is.

Italian flat bread with sage

CORIANDER CORN MUFFINS

Makes 8

These tasty muffins are deliciously spicy with a good hint of heat.

140g (4 ½oz/1 cup) cornmeal (polenta)
65g (2½oz) self-raising flour
½ tbsp baking powder
½ tsp salt
1 egg
50g (2oz/4 tbsp) butter
150ml (¼pt/⅔ cup) milk
¼ red or other mild onion, grated
2 dried chillies, crumbled
2 tbsp fresh coriander leaves, finely chopped

Preheat the oven to 200°C/400°F/Gas Mark 6. Sift all the dry ingredients together into a bowl. Gently melt the butter with some of the milk then add the remaining milk to cool down the mixture. Stir in the onion, chillies and coriander then whisk in the egg. Make a well in the dry ingredients and pour in the milk and egg mixture. Using a large metal spoon fold the ingredients together until just smooth and blended. Spoon into well greased bun tins about 4 cm (1½in) deep. Bake for 20 minutes. Serve warm.

HERB POPOVERS   *Makes 12*

butter or oil for greasing
3 eggs
250ml (8 fl oz/1 cup) milk
2 tbsp butter, melted
100g (3½oz/¾ cup) plain flour
pinch of salt
2 tbsp chopped mixed herbs such as chives, chervil, tarragon, dill and parsley or
  ½ tsp each of dried thyme and oregano

Liberally grease a bun tin with wells 4cm (1½ in) deep. Break the eggs into a bowl and mix them lightly. Whisk in the milk and melted butter and then whisk in the flour and salt until blended. Do not over mix. Stir in the fresh or dried herbs and half-fill the prepared wells with the batter. Place them in a cold oven. Turn the oven on to 220°C/425°F/Gas Mark 7 and bake for 30 minutes. Do not open the oven while the popovers are baking. If drier popovers are desired pierce each one with a knife after the 30 minutes baking time and bake a further 5 minutes. Serve at once while they are hot.

FIG AND THYME CHEWY BARS   *Makes about 48 bars*
Health conscious cooks will delight in this fat-free bar packed full of nutritious ingredients and most important of all – delicious to eat.

400g (14oz) dried figs
125g (4oz/⅝cup) demerrara (raw) sugar
2 tsp fresh lemon thyme leaves or 1 tsp dry thyme
75g (3oz/½ cup) chopped walnuts
125g (4oz/1 cup) plain flour
1 tsp baking powder
½ tsp cinnamon
¼ tsp ground cloves
¼ tsp ground mace or nutmeg
¼ tsp salt
3 eggs
2 tbsp brandy or cognac
icing (confectioners) sugar

Chop the figs roughly then place in a processor with some of the sugar and process to chop finely, or chop finely by hand. Mix with the remaining sugar, thyme and walnuts. Sift the flour, baking powder, spices and salt over the mixture and stir in. Stir in the lightly blended eggs and the brandy. Turn the mixture into a 20x30cm (8x10in) shallow tin lined with baking parchment. Bake in a preheated oven 170°C/325°F/Gas Mark 3 for 35-40 minutes. Leave in the tin for 5 minutes before turning out on to a sheet of greaseproof paper lightly sprinkled with icing sugar. Cut into bars when cold, store in an air-tight container.

Desserts

Melon and Grapes in Apple Mint Jelly
Serves 4

Although this sounds like a nursery pudding it is a deliciously refreshing way of serving fruit after a substantial dinner.

600ml (1pt/2½ cups) apple juice that is not made from a concentrate
juice of ½ lemon
50g (2oz/⅓ cup) sugar
1 melon and some grapes, or other fruit such as kiwi or mango
handful of fresh mint leaves
1 tbsp of gelatine

Place the apple juice, lemon juice and sugar in a saucepan and bring to the boil; throw in all but a few of the mint leaves, cover the pan and leave off the heat for a minute or two to infuse. Strain the juice. Place the gelatine in a small cup with 1 tbsp of cold water. Leave for a few minutes to sponge then set the cup in gently boiling water until the gelatine liquifies. Stir the gelatine into the apple juice. Pour the juice into a 900ml (1½ pt) bowl or divide it between 4 individual ramekins. Slice the fruit, arrange on top of the juice in a pretty pattern and decorate with a few of the reserved mint leaves. Refrigerate for at least 5 hours. This will make a very light set which will taste the nicest, but if you want to turn it out increase the gelatine by another ½ tbsp.

Poached Pears with Mint Sauce
Serves 6

300ml (½ pt/1¼ cups) water
75g (3oz/½ cup) sugar
juice and peel of 1 lemon
6 sprigs of mint plus 6 leaves
6 ripe Williams or Comice pears
150ml (¼ pt/⅔ cup) single cream
2 egg yolks

Bring the water, sugar, lemon juice and a few slivers of peel to the boil. Add the mint sprigs, remove from the heat and leave to infuse for several minutes. Taste before removing the mint to see if the flavour is strong

Fig and thyme chewy bars

enough. Peel the pears and cut them in half leaving on the stalks. Gently poach the pears in the syrup, covered, until they are just tender. Lift them out of the syrup and when cool remove the core and woody centre. Reduce the syrup to 150ml (¼ pt/⅔ cup). Whisk the egg yolks and cream together in a small bowl. Pour over the reduced syrup, whisking continuously, then pour the mixture back into the pan and stir over very low heat until the cream thickens slightly. Do not allow it to come near the boil. Adjust the

flavouring by adding more lemon juice, mint or sugar. Serve the pears with some sauce spooned over and garnished with a few finely shredded mint leaves.

GERANIUM CREAM WITH BLACKBERRIES

Serves 4

300ml (½ pt/1¼ cups) double cream
2 scented geranium leaves
2 tbsp sugar
500g (1 lb) blackberries

Place the cream with the sugar and geranium leaves in a double saucepan and heat, without boiling, for 15 minutes, or until the cream is well scented. Cool, then whip the cream and serve with the blackberries and additional sugar if needed.

BLACKCURRANT LEAF SORBET

Makes 900ml (1½ pt)

pared rind from 1 lemon
juice from 2-3 lemons
200g (7oz/1¼ cups) sugar
900ml (1½ pt/3½ cups) water
5 large handfuls of blackcurrant leaves
½ egg white

Place rind, sugar and water in a pan, bring to the boil and boil for 5 minutes. Add the washed leaves, cover the pan, and leave off the heat for 20 minutes. Strain the syrup, squeezing the leaves to extract all the flavour. Add half the lemon juice and taste before adding the rest. Freeze the mixture until half frozen. Whisk the egg white and stir a small amount into the sorbet. Continue to freeze until firm.

MINT TEA SORBET

Makes 900ml (1½pt)

900ml (1½pt) Earl Grey tea
200g (7oz/1¼ cups) sugar
4 large handfuls of mint leaves
juice of 1 lemon
juice of one orange
½ egg white, whisked

To garnish
crystallized mint leaves

Make the tea, infuse for 3 minutes and strain. Bring the tea and sugar to just below the boil, remove from the heat, add the mint, cover and leave to cool. Remove the mint and add the fruit juice. Place in a freezer until it is half frozen. Whisk in a small amount of the whisked egg white and freeze until firm. If the sorbet crystallizes and is too hard it can be cut into chunks and whizzed in a processor until smooth.

SCENTED GERANIUM
ICE CREAM
Makes 900ml (1½ pt)

Sorbets and ice creams need to be strongly flavoured because they lose some of their taste when they are frozen.

600ml (1 pt/2½ cups) milk
6 scented geranium leaves, bruised
2 eggs plus 2 egg yolks
75g (3oz/½ cup) caster sugar
150ml (¼ pt/⅔ cup) double cream

Scald the milk, remove from the heat and add the geranium leaves. Cover and leave to infuse for 20 minutes.

Whisk the eggs, egg yolks and sugar together. Remove the geranium leaves from the milk and reheat to just below the boil. Whisk a small amount of the hot milk on to the eggs, then pour the eggs back into the rest of the milk. Stir with a wooden spoon over low heat until the custard thickens. Do not allow it to come near the boil. Strain and when the custard is quite cool add the lightly whipped cream. Freeze in the usual way.

ROSE PETAL ICE CREAM
Serves 4-5

For this ice cream you will need very scented roses. Rugosas work very well and if you use a red variety such as *Roseraie de L'Hay* the ice cream will be a delicate peach colour.

petals from 4 highly scented rugosa roses
450ml (¾ pt/1 ½ cups) single cream
150ml (¼pt/½ cup) milk
75g (3oz/½ cup) sugar
3 egg yolks

Place petals, cream, milk and sugar in a heavy saucepan and heat slowly to just below the boil. Cover the pan and leave for 1 hour to infuse. Strain the mixture pressing the petals to extract the flavour. Reheat the cream to just below the boil again. Whisk the eggs in a small bowl. Whisk some of the hot cream on to the eggs then return the mixture to the pan and stir over very low heat until the custard thickens just enough to coat the spoon. Cool before setting in the freezer or ice cream maker. If using a freezer whisk the ice cream when it is half frozen to break up any crystals.

Rose petal ice cream

ELDERFLOWER FRITTERS

Makes 16

These are delicious served with stewed gooseberries or just on their own sprinkled with some sugar mixed with chopped sweet cicely.

For the batter
125g (4oz/1 cup) flour
pinch of salt
1 tbsp oil
150ml (¼ pt/⅔ cup) beer or water
2 small eggs, separated
2 heads of elderflowers per person
oil for deep frying
chopped sweet cicely (if available) mixed with a little sugar

Mix the flour and salt with the oil and beer or water, whisking well until smooth, then stir in the egg yolks. Cover and leave in a warm place for a few hours to allow the flour to ferment slightly. Before using whisk the egg whites until stiff and fold into the batter.

Heat the oil to 220°C/425°F. Shake the blossoms free of insects. Dip the heads into the batter and fry until golden brown. Serve sprinkled with sugar and chopped sweet cicely.

Ratafia Cream
Serves 8

This is an adapted version of a recipe from Hannah Glasse's *The Art of Cookery Made Plain and Easy*. Her successful book was first published in 1747 and it continued to be reprinted well into the nineteenth century.

900ml (1½ pt/4 cups) double cream
6 large bay leaves
2 eggs
3 egg yolks
4 tbsp caster sugar

Bring the cream and bay leaves slowly to the boil. When it reaches a good boil take the pan off the heat and remove the bay leaves. Whisk the eggs and egg yolks together with 4 tbsp of sugar. Whisk a little hot cream over the eggs then pour the egg mixture into the saucepan. Stir over very gentle heat until the custard thickens. Do not allow it to come near the boil. The custard will thicken further as it chills. Taste for flavouring. You may want to add more sugar or pop the bay leaves back to infuse further. Strain into ramekins, cool, then cover and refrigerate.

CHEESE AND HERB BUTTERS

Herb Cream Cheese

2-3 tbsp finely chopped mixed fresh herbs such as chervil, chives, tarragon and parsley
½ clove finely chopped garlic
225g (8oz) medium fat curd cheese, or sieved cottage cheese plus 3 tbsp double cream

Mix herbs and garlic into the cheese and wrap in cling-film forming a small wheel shape. Refrigerate until used.

Three Herb Cheese

175g (6oz) grated Cheddar cheese
3 tbsp double cream
4 tbsp dry sherry
2-3 tbsp chopped mixed fresh chervil, chives and winter savory

Stir all the ingredients together, in the top of a double saucepan set over simmering water, until blended. Pot, cover and refrigerate. Use within 10 days.

BORAGE CHEESE

250g (8oz) fresh ricotta cheese or sieved cottage cheese plus 2 tbsp of double cream
a good handful of very young borage leaves, very finely chopped
1 tbsp finely chopped fresh dill
borage flowers

Mix the cheese with the chopped borage leaves and dill, form into a round shape and decorate with lots of borage flowers.

HERB BUTTERS

Herb butters can be kept frozen ready to be sliced and used on grilled meat, in stuffings, or on pasta or bread. All kinds of fresh herbs can be used – whatever is in season. The amount to use depends on the herb but a rough guide is 4-5 tbsp of a finely chopped herb to 225g (8oz) of butter. Chervil, basil or coriander make delicious herb butters and parsley with finely chopped garlic is also very good. Be sure to use salted butter.

Chop the herb very finely and blend with the butter (can be done in a food processor). Place on cling-film and form into a long rectangle. Chill in the refrigerator, then cut into lengths and wrap tightly in foil. Label and freeze.

VINEGARS AND OILS

HERB VINEGARS

An excellent all-purpose vinegar which can be used immediately is made by bringing 2.2l (4pt) of cider vinegar to the boil, removing it from the heat and adding several sprigs each of tarragon, thyme, parsley and marjoram, 4 bay leaves, 6 cloves of garlic crushed but unpeeled and 4 branches of savory. Cover and leave overnight then strain. A sprig of thyme or tarragon can be added to the bottles before sealing.

ELDERFLOWER VINEGAR

This is particularly good for marinades or meat salads. Pull off the flowers from about 30 elderflower blossoms using a fork. Discard the stalks and leave the blossoms overnight on paper to dry. Place them in 2¼ l (4 pt) of vinegar. Leave for 3-4 weeks before straining.

HERB OILS

The aromatic flavour of herbs can be imparted to oils by leaving them in the oils for several weeks. Several good sprigs of basil in 300ml (½ pt) of olive oil makes a delicious oil to use in the winter months when basil is

Herb butters

HOLLY BUSH
Finest Quality Butter

HOLLY BUSH BUTTER

Elderflower champagne

unavailable. A general herb oil can be made by placing 3 sprigs each of tarragon and thyme, 1 garlic clove, a small dried hot chilli and a few peppercorns in 600ml (1 pt) of sunflower or groundnut oil.

DRINKS

ICED MINT TEA

This is an enormously popular summer drink in America. It is both refreshing and energizing.

Pour 6 cups of good strong hot tea into a jug. Add 4 bruised sprigs of mint and the juice of one lime. Leave to infuse for half an hour then strain. Serve in tall glasses with ice, slices of lime, and sprigs of fresh mint. Sweeten with caster sugar as desired.

ELDERFLOWER CHAMPAGNE *Makes 4 l (1 gall)*

4l (1gall) water
625g (1¼ lb/2½ cups) sugar
4 large heads of elderflowers
2 lemons
2 tbsp mild white wine vinegar

Boil the water, pour over the sugar and stir to dissolve. When the syrup is cool add the elderflowers, juice of one lemon, slices from the other and vinegar. Cover with a cloth and leave for 24 hours. Strain through a fine sieve squeezing the flowers to extract all the flavour. Store in screw-topped bottles. The champagne will be ready after 10 days. Drink within 3-4 weeks.

JELLIES

SCENTED GERANIUM JELLY

Never turn down apple windfalls, they can provide the base for a variety of delicious herb jellies. Scented geraniums make a fragrant jelly delicious with cold meat or with cream cheese. Tarragon jelly is particularly good with chicken and parsley jelly goes very well with game.

2¼ kg (5lb) tart cooking or crab apples
juice of 2 lemons
14 scented geranium leaves
sugar

Wash the apples, remove any blemishes, cut into quarters and place in a large saucepan. Add just enough water to barely cover the fruit and simmer very gently, covered, until the apples have become a soft pulp. Turn out into a jelly bag and leave to drain overnight.

Measure 450g (1lb) of sugar for each 600ml (1pt/2½ cups) of apple juice and set aside. Place the apple juice, lemon juice and 10 geranium leaves in a preserving pan and boil for 15 minutes. Meanwhile warm the sugar in a very low oven. Add the warmed sugar to the preserving pan, stirring to dissolve, and boil for 3 minutes. Test for setting by putting a spoonful of jelly on a plate and cooling in the refrigerator. Remove the leaves and discard. Place a small fresh leaf in the bottom of each sterilised jar, ladle in the jelly and cover with waxed discs at once. Cover with a lid later, and label.

TARRAGON JELLY

Follow the above method but use 5 tbsp of fresh chopped tarragon leaves in place of the geranium leaves. Strain the jelly, add another tablespoon of fresh chopped tarragon leaves and bottle.

MINT JELLY

Substitute a bunch of mint and a wine glass of mild vinegar for the geranium leaves. Remove the mint after it has boiled for a few minutes, tasting to ensure the right strength of flavour.

PARSLEY JELLY

Substitute a large bunch of parsley for the geranium leaves. Strain the jelly and add some finely chopped parsley before bottling.

THYME JELLY

Substitute a few sprigs of thyme for the geranium leaves. Strain the jelly and add some finely chopped fresh thyme leaves to the jelly before bottling.

Herb jellies

Melon and grapes in apple jelly

EXTRAS

CRYSTALLIZED FLOWERS

(see frontispiece)

Rose petals, violets, primroses, pinks and fruit or herb flowers can be crystallized as well as mint leaves.

Whisk an egg white until it is very frothy. Use a brush to paint each petal, flower or leaf on both sides with the egg white. Then carefully sprinkle or dip lightly in caster sugar. Place on a wire tray and dry in a warm oven with the door ajar.

Another method is to mix 1 small tsp of gum tragacanth with 2 tbsp of rose water and use in place of the egg white. This will give a more professional finish.

LAVENDER SUGAR

Lavender sugar can be used to make ice cream or to flavour puddings or biscuits. The sugar will be very fragrant so use with caution, replacing only a small amount of the sugar required in a recipe with lavender sugar. Pick the lavender when it is just coming into flower, before it is in full bloom. Spread it out to dry then remove the stalks and discard by running your fingers down the stalk from top to bottom. Blend or process with 4 times their weight in sugar. Spread out to dry for a few hours before pouring into air-tight jars. Rose petals or mint can also be used to flavour sugar by the same method.

INDEX